CALL CENTER RECRUITING AND NEW-HIRE TRAINING

The Best of
Call Center Management Review

Call Center Press
A Division of ICMI, Inc.

Published by
Call Center Press
A Division of ICMI, Inc.
P.O. Box 6177
Annapolis, Maryland 21401

Design by Ellen K. Herndon

Contents

Foreword

The highest hurdle that stands before most call center managers today is the shortage of qualified agents. The increase in call center openings, low employment and intense rivalry for multiskilled agents will add up (if it doesn't already) to a management nightmare unless you have an effective recruitment and new-hire training program in place.

To help you prepare for booming call center growth and the demands of the emerging multichannel environment, we have compiled a collection of articles, ideas and tools to give you the foundation for a forward-thinking approach to agent recruitment and new-hire training. In these pages, you will find innovative practices, programs and strategies to get the right people with the right aptitudes and abilities in place before training commences… and then cultivate those new hires into high-performance agents equipped and ready for the challenges ahead.

We hope you enjoy the book!

Sincerely,
The ICMI Team

Chapter 1:
Managers' Views on Staffing

Call Center Managers Share Secrets at Human Resources Roundtable

Guide to Call Center Staffing Success in the New Millennium

Call Center Managers Share Secrets at Human Resources Roundtable

by Greg Levin

A frigid day in February 1996 soon heated up as directors, managers and supervisors from three Midwest call centers addressed hot human resources issues, such as hiring, training, motivation, career-pathing and turnover.

The event, organized by Jon Anton, director of the Center for Customer-Driven Quality at Purdue University in West Lafayette, Indiana, included participants from Norrell Staffing Services (who handle all hiring and training for Thomson Consumer Electronics' call center in Indianapolis); Ruppman Marketing Technology in Peoria, Illinois; and Osram Sylvania Inc. in Westfield, Indiana. Participants began their discussion at Thomson's headquarters and later moved to Sylvania's call center just a few miles down the road.

"The idea [for the roundtable] began after a discussion with some of the Ruppman call center people about their human resource challenges, which included a 40 percent annual turnover rate," explains Anton. "I thought it would be a good idea to organize a day of human resource benchmarking to see if other call center managers would be willing to share any secrets."

We're Talking Turnover

Turnover turned out to be the most recurrent subject of the day because it is intertwined in nearly all human resources topics. While the three call centers approach turnover in different ways due to a diverse range of factors specific to each company, including job complexity, career paths and local competition, all agreed that call centers that struggle the least always seem to have one thing in common: employees who are involved in decision-making processes.

"Organizations with the lowest turnover are those whose employees are empowered to make decisions and who don't spend each day merely passing calls through and taking information," said Tracy Pitcher, call center manager at Thomson Electronics.

One attendee acknowledged that one area in her call center has high turnover because of the repetitive nature of the calls. "Sounds like an easy job, but that's exactly the problem — it's redundant," she said. "People don't like to be in that position very long."

Another attendee said the only thing that caused more contention than turnover itself was how it should be measured. While there is no standard equation for calculating turnover, all were impressed by a formula used by Bobbie Adams, human resources manager for Osram Sylvania, a leading manufacturer of electronic products. She takes the number of "separations" — or employees who have left the company — for each month, divides that number by the average number of employees on payroll during that month, and multiplies the quotient by 100 percent.

This formula not only determines a turnover rate on a monthly (rather than annual) basis, it also discounts those employees who are promoted within the company. "We consider it a positive thing for the company as a whole whenever somebody leaves to take a job someplace else within the organization," said Adams. "We don't factor that in when trying to determine turnover."

That point led to a discussion of the positive aspects of turnover. "Rather than worry about turnover all the time, plan for it," Anton advised, pointing out that some turnover is natural and even desirable. Once a worker maxes out or reaches the top of his or her position, if that person stays there for much longer, their productivity will inevitably decline. Kris Shallenberger, account manager at Thomson, agreed, pointing out how she and the other managers at Thomson keep such drops in individual productivity in check. "We actually try to 'force' turnover in some instances," she explained. "We follow [veteran] employees' productivity very closely,

---

Sylvania's Turnover Equation

$$\frac{\text{number of separations during the month}}{\text{average number of employees on the payroll that month}} \times 100\%$$

Chapter 1

and when we start to see it dip down, we realize it may be time for that person to move up to a different position." She added that when there is no more room for promotions or lateral moves, turnover naturally occurs.

Relying on Recruiting and Hiring

One of the biggest challenges many technical call centers face is finding phone reps who have a good balance of technical and customer service skills. While training can provide some skills in this area, it's better if the rep has some of these skillsets at the time of hire. As one attendee said, "Originally, we hired all technical people, but their customer service skills were poor. Then we hired a group of customer service specialists, but they ended up talking around many of the customer's technical problems. It's difficult to find that magical mix of somebody who embodies both technical and customer service savvy."

To try to find such a mix, these call center managers focus on effective recruiting methods. Some participants suggested networking with instructors at local trade and business schools or community colleges to gain an edge in recruiting qualified call center personnel. "We treat some of the instructors at these schools like clients," said Shallenberger. "We want to establish a solid rapport with them so that they will continue to give us good referrals for our call center."

Another effective recruiting method discussed by participants was employee referrals. One attendee's center offers bonuses and incentives to employees who provide referrals that lead to a hiring.

In addition to recruiting methods, participants discussed how they screen and test call center applicants. Shallenberger described Thomson's prescreening phone interview, which consists of about 10 questions including "How did you find out about us?" and "What is your job history?" These general questions are followed by call-center specific role-playing inquiries. "We give them a hypothetical situation and ask them how they would handle it," explained Shallenberger. "We like to see how they respond on the spot."

Applicants who pass the prescreening call are invited to the center for a written test and interview designed to assess technical, logical and vocabulary skills. "Based on their testing and interview results, we tell applicants where in our center we think they would be most successful, or if we feel they may be better off working somewhere else," Shallenberger said.

The Ruppman call center uses a similar screening and interviewing process, emphasizing keyboard skills from the onset, said Susan Stratton, Ruppman manager. "I have applicants use the keyboard right off the bat to assess their skills. Applicants often say they have computer/keyboard skills, but in reality they struggle."

Attendees also discussed the challenges involved with hiring people with special needs. Several participants who employ students and young mothers to work part-time struggle with scheduling issues. "It's sometimes difficult to work around these employees' needs," says Stratton. "Between students' classes and mothers' daycare issues, our schedules run all over the board and we're not always sure we are staffing appropriately with regard to call volume."

The Thomson call center tries to tackle such issues during the hiring process, assigning individuals specific time slots. "That way they know what's expected and if they come to me later and say, 'I can't work this time,' I can say, 'But in the interview you said you could,'" explained manager Pitcher. "Hiring for specific time slots gives me the reassurance of coverage and the employee a consistent schedule that won't disrupt their lives."

Sending a Message via Training

Effective training programs not only prepare new reps for success and help to improve existing reps' performance, they send a message to employees that they are important investments, participants agreed. And this positive message enhances employee motivation and retention. "Whether it's initial training, followup training or cross-training, if people feel that you are investing something in them, they are going to work harder and stay with you longer," said Shallenberger.

The Ruppman call center attendees develop highly qualified reps through a new mentoring program. Since introducing the program, which involves lead reps ("mentors") working side-by-side with and helping to enhance the skills of newer employees, Ruppman's Stratton claims the center has enjoyed tremendous benefits, including productivity increases, a reduction in the time it takes new reps to "get on the phones" from six weeks to two, job enrichment for lead reps and the opportunity for new employees to make a friend immediately after being hired.

New reps learn at their own speed, says Stratton, initially listening to their mentor take calls and asking questions in between customers.

Stratton acknowledges that mentoring takes an initial small toll on lead rep productivity, but says that the sacrifice is well worth it.

"Because lead reps must stop between calls and explain things to new reps, there's a small tradeoff on the lead reps' productivity for the first four or five days," she explained. "But the new employees are now on the phones taking calls within two weeks, which more than makes up for any loss in the early stages of the mentoring process. And both the existing and the newer employees love the program!"

Another attendee discussed how her center uses cross-training to develop a pool of reps who can handle a wide variety of call types and other tasks. One attendee commended these cross-training efforts, but offered a friendly warning. "When it comes to cross-training, you can take a good thing way too far," she said. "My call center found this out the hard way. We decided to cross-train our reps in order to maximize efficiency, and many burned out quickly." The group agreed that there is a fine line between effective cross-training and knowledge overload. "You have to take a look at your staff and decide what will work best for them," said one attendee. "You don't want to send them too many simple calls because they will burn out from boredom. But you also don't want to overload them either."

Maintaining Motivation

Career-pathing and incentives/motivation were additional hot topics discussed by participants.

"We hire 'true' customer service reps [for the consumer relations department], people with good listening and typing skills, perhaps with call center experience," Shallenberger explained. "We're not hiring electronic wizards for that department, so there is not a lot of room for movement in our company. That's why we've gotten creative with the career path here. We've set up different tiers for those employees to

Chapter 1

help keep them motivated. Sometimes it's just a lateral move, but it's often enough to help keep them here longer."

Sylvania uses a variety of incentive programs to "keep reps there longer," said Adams. In addition to using a pay-for-performance plan to determine employee raises, Sylvania sponsors a Perfect Attendance Award. For each year a rep has a perfect attendance record, he or she receives $500. Since implementing the attendance award three years ago, tardiness is down 40.5 percent and absenteeism is down 25.6 percent. "We may pay a lot out in attendance incentives, but we save even more because our calls get answered efficiently and we have fewer employee sick days to cover."

Other incentives and benefits mentioned by participants included tuition reimbursement programs, daycare facilities and even massage sessions for employees.

We Should Do This More Often

By the end of the day, everybody was excited to take what they had learned back to their call centers. And the organizer, Anton, was excited about the level of intensity that was maintained by all throughout the day.

"I was overwhelmed by how open and frank people were about personnel issues at their operations," he says. "Every call center manager shares the goal of filling workstations with good people. After seeing these participants' commitment to and pride in what they are doing at their call centers, I realized how important it is for more and more managers to come together and address the challenges we addressed."

Guide to Call Center Staffing Success in the New Millennium

by Greg Levin

While visions of the 21st century historically have featured robots and cars that hover, the dominant issues and challenges for call centers in the new millennium revolve around ordinary people. The highest hurdle that stands before most managers today is the shortage of qualified agents caused by booming call center growth and competition.

In a reader survey conducted by *Call Center Management Review* in late 1999, staffing was identified as far and away the biggest call center concern for today's managers. And it isn't going to get any easier in the near future, as call centers are poised for even more tremendous growth over the next several years (i.e., studies show that the number of North American centers will increase by well over 50 percent by 2003), which will further deplete agent resources.

This article explores what we at *Call Center Management Review* feel are the most creative and innovative staffing practices, programs and strategies that call center professionals should consider to ensure their centers' survival — at least until Buck Rogers arrives to take things over.

1. Establish a staff-sharing alliance with a compatible call center. "It'll never work!" "It's too risky!" "Nobody's doing it!" These are the usual reactions whenever staff-sharing is suggested to call center professionals. Well, it can work and it doesn't have to be risky.

Staff-sharing refers to when two call centers with complementary busy seasons form a staffing alliance to help each center cost-effectively handle its workload. For instance, let's say call center A's peak season occurs November through February, and call center B's occurs April through July. The two centers — provided they are relatively close geographically, have no competitive links to one another and pay staff roughly the same salary — could switch a dedicated pool of agents back and forth among them, depending on the season.

Such an alliance enables both centers to manage peaks and valleys without having to continually hire — and then lay off — seasonal temps. It also adds diversity to agents' jobs and offers them a unique opportunity that could entice them to stick around both centers for a long time.

The best-known example of a staff-sharing venture was carried out by WearGuard Corporation — a clothing manufacturer — and Cross Country Group, which handles roadside assistance calls for car manufacturers and insurance companies. The program, which involved 35 agents from each center, was deemed a success by both companies, though it ended a year and a half later when Cross Country outgrew the arrangement and decided to open a second call center.

While few similar alliances currently exist, numerous call centers — realizing the severe extent of today's staffing challenge — are looking into staff-sharing as a viable option. Find them and form a unique alliance!

2. Use former agents as peak-season/contingency staff. While retaining agents should be a major priority of call center managers, moderate staff attrition is virtually unavoidable at most companies. Many of the best agents move on to other areas within the company to help advance their careers. Several innovative call centers have found ways to continue tapping into their most talented agents, taking advantage of their unique knowledge and experience even after they've moved on.

For example, People's Bank's call center in Bridgeport, Connecticuit, uses former agents — who now work in marketing, accounting, etc. — to help out on the phones during peak periods. The call center loves the arrangement because it enables them to manage seasonal call spikes without having to hire and train temporary staff. And the former agents love it because it gives them the opportunity to earn additional money. (They typically handle calls in the evening and on weekends to avoid interference with their current jobs.)

The Hartford Customer Services Group (HCSG) uses a similar staffing approach at its call center in Fort Washington, Pennsylvania. "Former agents serve as very valuable contingency staff for us. I don't know how we'd get through our peak periods without them," says Jay Minnucci, director of call center operations for HCSG.

In addition to helping to cost-effectively manage dynamic call volumes, the use of former agents now working in other areas can enhance communication and working relationships between the call center and various departments within the company.

3. Set up shop in less-saturated call center locations. While the two practices above can be very effective, they won't always be viable solutions for call centers that struggle with base staffing due to regional call center saturation. If this describes your situation, you may want to talk to senior management about setting up an additional center in a less-saturated geographic area.

Several growing companies have successfully overcome their staffing woes in crowded and competitive urban areas by establishing call centers in smaller suburban and rural areas. Many of these locations offer a relatively large skilled labor force and moderate to high unemployment due to a shortage of diverse industry in the area. This means they are prime for the picking by call centers hungry for talented and trainable staff.

Hilton Reservations Worldwide has significantly eased its staffing stress by establishing call centers in two such towns. In 1996, the hotel chain began searching for additional sites to supplement its Dallas center, which was struggling to find the agents it needed to handle an increasing workload. Hilton opted to set up shop in Hazletown, Pennsylvania, a mill town with ample resources and with no other call centers to compete for agents.

"When we first started recruiting, we received 500 applications for the first 100 jobs, and most of the candidates had good skills and a very strong work ethic," says Kim King, former manager of the Hazletown site. Today, King heads up Hilton's new call center in another lesser-known town — Hemet, California. The company opened the Hemet site after seeing how successful the Hazletown center was from a staffing and costs perspective.

So far, things are going just as smoothly in Hemet — the center received nearly 1,000 applications for the first 100 jobs.

Is King concerned that, by sharing information about her company's prime call center "finds," other companies will move into town and spoil things? Not really. She points out that Hazletown and Hemet are just two out of hundreds of towns that Hilton found during its searches that are ideal for call centers looking to overcome their staffing droughts.

4. Tap into the disabled labor pool. Establishing a telecommuting program for home-based disabled agents can be a potentially powerful staffing solution for your call center. Call centers shouldn't hire disabled individuals just because it's a socially responsible thing to do, but because it is a smart thing to do from a staffing standpoint. The disabled — particularly those who are home-based — represent a highly underutilized labor pool. Most are perfectly suited for the agent position, which usually doesn't require much physical mobility.

Many home-based disabled workers — tired of dead-end, mindless jobs — are hungry for challenging work in a booming industry like call centers that offers ample room for advancement. Not only is there an abundant supply of home-based disabled workers who are well suited for call center work, turnover among them is typically very low due to the limited employment opportunities available to them in the overall job market, according to M.J. Willard, executive director of the National Telecommuting Institute (NTI), a Boston-based nonprofit organization that seeks employment for physically disabled individuals who require home-based work.

Willard adds that government agencies will often provide ample financial support to assist companies that hire home-based disabled workers. "Think about what you spend on recruiting, training and equipment," she says. "If you use disabled telecommuters as agents, it's possible to have an outside agency pick up the tab for these expenses... Call center work is clearly part of the wave of the future for home-based disabled workers." (You can read more about recruiting disabled workers in Chapter 6.)

5. Partner with local colleges that have call center/customer service programs. There has been an emergence of call center programs created by colleges in response to the need for qualified agents in local centers. Most of these programs provide extensive classroom and hands-on agent training (over 700 hours at some schools), and focus on promoting call center careers — not just short-term jobs — for students (see "College Call Center Programs Help to Fill Shallow Labor Pool," in Chapter 2).

Partnering with one or more of these schools to help them develop and maintain their call center programs may prove fruitful from both a staffing and cost-savings standpoint. First of all, the schools typically give their partners first pick of recent "agent graduates." Not only can this save your center significantly on recruiting costs, the quality of the candidates is often higher than what you'll find "on the streets."

"We've hired agents who've graduated from the call center training program at the College de l'Outaouais [in Quebec]," explains Ann Lapalice, manager of the Canadian Medical Pro-

> **Millennium Staffing Guide at a Glance**
>
> 1. Establish a staff-sharing alliance with a compatible call center.
> 2. Use former agents as peak-season/contingency staff.
> 3. Set up shop in less-saturated call center locations.
> 4. Tap into the disabled labor pool.
> 5. Partner with local colleges that have call center/customer service programs.
> 6. Use employment agencies specializing in call center staffing.
> 7. Link to cyber agents.
> 8. Outsource Web-based customer support to Net rep specialists.

tection Association's call center. "We like to hire these graduates because they're already trained on computer applications, telephone etiquette, etc. They're ready to take on the job of call center agent." Because graduates are so well prepared in the program, the time and money spent on training them once hired can be reduced significantly. A week of company-specific product/service training is often all that these agents need before handling calls in your center.

6. Use employment agencies specializing in call center staffing. Most call center managers don't have enough free time to aggressively recruit agents and promote the growing opportunities in call center work to job seekers. The good news is that several of today's largest employment agencies do. Well-known agencies, such as Manpower and Olsten Staffing Services, have established specific programs that focus solely on staffing resources for call centers worldwide, particularly in areas of high call center concentration where staffing is most challenging. Depending on a call center client's needs, these agencies can provide everything from assistance with agent recruiting and evaluation to complete on-site management of call center staff. (See "Call Center Managers Turn to Employment Specialists for Staffing Solutions," in Chapter 2.)

Staffing agencies can help you to find good agents fast, but you have to take time to evaluate several agencies to determine which is most compatible with your call center's needs and budget. You also have to understand exactly what skills, experience levels and personality types you seek in agents, and be able to clearly communicate those criteria to the agency.

And be sure to closely evaluate all agent candidates provided by the agency. Don't assume that because you are dealing with a professional service, you can rush through the staffing process. If you do, you'll likely up with the same poor service levels you had back when you were understaffed.

7. Link to cyber agents. What if you had access to a nationwide network of remote agents — fully trained at no expense to your call center — to whom you could route calls during peak periods and pay only when used?

That's the idea behind the "CyberAgent Network," a unique staffing network operated by Miami-based Willow CSN that links call center clients to a pool of independent work-at-home agents certified to handle calls for up to five or six companies each day (www.willowcsn.com).

Call centers can use Willow's CyberAgents on both a "scheduled" and "on-call" basis to help manage call spikes, staff shortages and crisis situations. And because CyberAgents work out of their homes, you can use agents outside of your local labor pool, thus extending your call center's recruiting reach significantly. Willow currently has more than 2,000 CyberAgents located primarily in South Florida and New York, but hopes to have a much larger pool located nationwide in the future.

While still in an extended growth stage (Willow has been claiming for years that the network will revolutionize the industry), the CyberAgent Network has recently attracted several clients and could have a profound impact on the nature of call center staffing as we know it.

"Since the beginning, I've felt that Willow may be on to something big," says Nancy Hammond, former vice president of customer service for the Signature

Group — a marketing company that uses more than 200 CyberAgents to supplement its staff of 900 inhouse agents. "The real test will be how the network handles all the growth that is expected in the near future."

8. Outsource Web-based customer support to Net rep specialists. Finding call center agents with solid customer service skills, sales skills and computer savvy is hard enough in today's job market; add writing skills to the list and you've just shrunk the needle while increasing the size of the haystack.

Many call centers are in a tight spot; they recognize the demand for solid Web-based customer support (particularly via email and live text-chat) — and are anxious to provide such support — but struggle to find agents with the right skill sets.

To overcome this challenge, some call centers have recently started outsourcing their Web-based customer transactions to a new breed of service bureau. These unique "e-sourcing" agencies are staffed with trained Net reps who specialize in handling email inquiries and providing support via text-chat sessions for client companies.

In addition to enhancing online service and customer satisfaction, e-sourcing agencies have the staff needed to close e-commerce sales that are often lost by companies that don't (or struggle to) provide agent support via their Web sites. Companies like florist KaBloom can attest to that. KaBloom recently contracted with e-sourcer eSupportNow, whose Net reps handle all email and chat sessions that originate from the flower company's Web site (www.kabloom.com).

"We definitely have an edge using a team of agents dedicated to answering customers' online requests and bringing Web-based sales to completion," says David Hartstein, president of KaBloom. "eSupportNow's staff does a great job providing the kind of customer support that we aren't so adept at."

Avoid Millennium Migraines

Call center staffing issues will continue to cause migraines among managers who don't embrace creative and innovative strategies. The call center boom keeps booming, the traditional agent pools keep draining and the demands of customers keep increasing.

You can continue with a business-as-usual approach to staffing in an industry that's rapidly becoming "business unusual," or you can implement some of the ideas listed above and enter the new millennium with a powerful frontline force.

Chapter 1

Chapter 2:
Recruiting

How to Develop a Retention-Oriented Agent Recruiting and Selection Process

by Anita O'Hara

Managers in this people-intensive business of customer care are aware that their employee costs generally comprise about 80 percent of a typical operating budget. Did you know that, by focusing solely on cutting your attrition by two percentage points per month, you could reduce your operating expenses by almost 10 percent? Not only that, you'll also reap additional benefits, such as improved customer satisfaction through more consistent customer service and higher employee satisfaction.

That sounds like a great payback, doesn't it? And yet, so much easier to say than to do.

So what's the secret? Managers need to work at viewing agent retention from a holistic standpoint. It's not enough to have retention-oriented team leaders on board who regularly incent and recognize agent performance with contests and special events. It's not enough to develop a solid training approach or a rich career path process.

Instead, success is a combination of all of these things, or in other words, in creating a solid retention program from the start — when the agent joins the call center — through every single "moment of truth" that involves the agent.

The "retention wheel," on page 22, illustrates all of the areas to focus on, which are key to creating a solid plan. This article will focus on the first step, recruitment and selection.

There are six fundamental steps in the recruitment and selection process:

1. Analyze job tasks.
2. Identify specific skills and competencies required.
3. Describe the performance required by the job.
4. Develop a job description.
5. Identify source pools and a recruitment plan.
6. Define and implement your selection process.

Analyzing Job Tasks

The first two steps can be completed concurrently. Begin by taking a detailed look at your top-performing agents. Consider both the efficiency and effectiveness with which they perform their tasks. It may also be useful to re-review your star agents' resumes. Also, take the time to observe and conduct followup interviews with a group of "experts" performing their jobs. Try to identify common tasks they perform well.

Use this analysis to create a list of skills that are critical, such as communication and articulation, analytical skills, organizational skills (talk and type/overlapping), call center or customer service experience, listening skills and computer skills.

If you are creating a customer service organization from the ground up, and have no stars from which to create a standard, try benchmarking with a similar type of company. Generally, you'll find that, regardless of industry, call center managers are looking for agents with similar skills.

Next, consider which competencies or behaviors you want your prospective employees to demonstrate. A few common competencies include positive attitude,

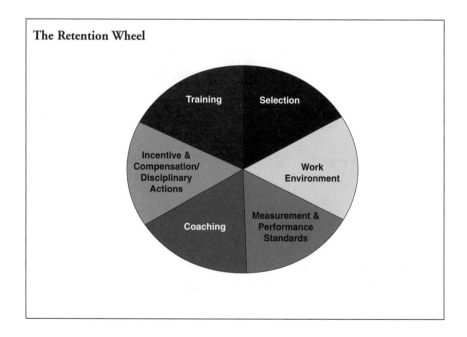

The Retention Wheel

Training
Selection
Incentive & Compensation/ Disciplinary Actions
Work Environment
Coaching
Measurement & Performance Standards

Chapter 2

flexibility, teamwork and cooperation, customer orientation, self-reliance and stamina. There are a variety of companies that can help you to identify these, and that can even create a hiring instrument that will improve your retention rates.

Writing a Job Description Aimed at High Performance

Once you know what type of agent you're looking for, you can identify the type of performance required and write your job description. At this stage, you're prioritizing your desired and required skills and competencies, describing the work environment in which employees will coexist, identifying the scope and breadth of the job (e.g., what kinds of decisions will prospective agents make?).

In addition, this is the point at which you should identify the agents' pay structure. It's best to include two key groups in this process:

- **Human resources** can help to assess compensation in the external market. They can also help to price your jobs comparable to other jobs within the organization.
- **The senior leadership team** can help you to identify your pay strategy. That is, do you want to be the employer of choice or simply pay the market average?

Finding Staff Sources

Every staff selection strategy should include recruitment sources as well as a selection plan. It's important to track your sources and analyze their success over time. For each candidate hired, be sure to track and record the following: 1) source, 2) performance, 3) attendance record, and 4) tenure.

In this manner, you can determine the success of each source. If one source yields consistently high-performing agents who stay, keep using it. If, on the other hand, a source results in an agent pool that regularly turns over, it's time to stop recruiting through that source. Following are a few common recruitment sources:

- **Employee referrals** — from the top-performing agents who fit well into your work environment.
- **Advertising** — in local newspapers or trade publications.
- **College recruitment** — works best with part-time staff, preferably with a good

tuition reimbursement program as a benefit.

- **Physically challenged** — check to see if there is a state program that will work with your center to assess the environment and help to curtail the costs of special equipment.

- **Career fairs by invitation** — be sure to publicize it widely. Have candidates send resumes in advance. Call prescreened candidates to invite them (or not) to your event. Be sure to set up interview rooms in advance for interviews and/or role-play exercises.

- **Internet** — candidates who browse recruiting Web sites are likely to be Internet savvy.

Defining and Implementing a Selection Process

Finally, the last step is to define and implement your selection process. There are a variety of tools that you can employ in this process.

It's important to carefully consider the sequence of these events. For instance, the

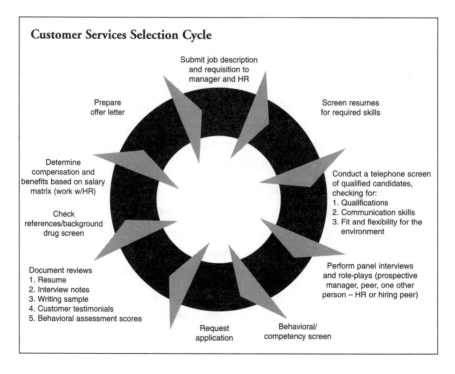

Customer Services Selection Cycle

Submit job description and requisition to manager and HR

Prepare offer letter

Screen resumes for required skills

Determine compensation and benefits based on salary matrix (work w/HR)

Conduct a telephone screen of qualified candidates, checking for:
1. Qualifications
2. Communication skills
3. Fit and flexibility for the environment

Check references/background drug screen

Document reviews
1. Resume
2. Interview notes
3. Writing sample
4. Customer testimonials
5. Behavioral assessment scores

Perform panel interviews and role-plays (prospective manager, peer, one other person – HR or hiring peer)

Request application

Behavioral/ competency screen

"customer services selection cycle," on page 24, illustrates a sample process.

The most common pitfall for managers during the final selection is to put too much weight on a single facet of the screening/interview process. For instance, a candidate may be terrified by the job interview, yet have an excellent background, great references, and good scores on the behavioral screen, and he may have presented himself in an excellent fashion during the phone screen. Consider all parts of the process, as well as the weight you will attach to each, before making your final selection.

As you can see, a lot of work goes into an effective agent recruitment and selection process — from brainstorming and describing your ideal call center agent all the way to the sequence and timing of the final selection process. But if you take the time to plan your strategy well, it will start with selecting a star performer and end with retaining one!

Chapter 2

Recruiting Strategies
for Multimedia Call Centers

by Greg Levin

While advanced technology has certainly enhanced today's call center capabilities, there is no argument that agents are still the most important resource for call center success. Unfortunately, there is also no argument that finding those crucial resources is getting more difficult.

According to the Customer Contact Strategy Forum — a Toronto-based association for North American call center executives, recruiting skilled staff is, by far, the biggest challenge for today's call center manager. "Our members come in all the time saying they can't find people," says Sarah Kennedy, president of the forum. "The skill demand in the call center industry is going through the roof."

True, higher customer expectations and new customer contact channels — particularly email and the Web — have certainly raised the bar for agent recruiting. But top call centers are learning that, by adding ample muscle to their hiring strategies, finding agents who can handle the multimedia blitz doesn't have to be a Herculean task.

The problem is that many multimedia call centers are still using the same tired recruiting techniques they used back when traditional phone agents were all they needed. They have done little to attract and attain the type of staff they need today — agents with the skills to effectively handle the customer email and Web-based transactions now flowing into the center.

In Search of Net Reps

While everybody is talking about how crucial Net reps are today, few are talking about how to find them. According to Wanda Sitzer, cofounder and executive vice president of Initiatives Three, a consulting firm specializing in phone and Web initiatives to improve customer support, managers in search of quality Net reps need to go through a formal process that includes four essential steps.

• **Define Net rep requirements.** Before you can begin looking for Net reps, you have to know exactly what you're looking for. A Net rep at one call center may have quite different responsibilities than a Net rep at another. It's up to you to carefully define the position: Will they handle email only or Web-chat, as well? Will they also handle voice-based transactions online, e.g., voice over Internet protocol (VoIP) and/or Web callbacks? Do they need page-push and/or collaborative browsing skills? Will they be primarily sales, service or tech support agents? Does (or will) video come into play at your center?

The answers to these questions will serve as the guide to your entire Net rep hiring process. Without it, it's easy to get lost during the "e-cruiting" and skills assessment stages.

• **Implement a progressive "e-cruiting" strategy.** Placing traditional employment ads in the local newspaper is not the best way to find top online agents. To find candidates with the written and technical skills you're seeking, you need to recruit using the same medium in which agents will be working — the Web. Post Net agent job openings on your corporate Web site and intranet (for recruiting internally), as well as on at least one of the growing number of online career centers and recruiting sites that exist on the Web today.

"Applicants who search sites like ours demonstrate Net savvy — a good start when looking for online reps," says Tara Thorne of Web recruiter CareerBuilder. There are even a few online recruiting sites dedicated specifically to call centers, such as CallCenterCareers.com. In addition, several call center consultancy Web sites now feature pages where companies can post job openings.

Encourage all Net rep applicants to respond to online job ads via email, and take note of those who comply with these instructions. "If candidates call to ask about the job, you may have just learned their preferred communication style — vocal, not written — and they may not be the right person for the Net agent job," Sitzer points out. Be sure to include a detailed job description as part of your online ad to ensure that applicants are aware of the skills they'll need to succeed.

Applicants who follow the online application procedure, who have no problem attaching documents (i.e., resume, cover letter) and who demonstrate good writing

skills should be invited to participate in the next phase of the hiring process.

• **Assess candidates' customer support skills online.**
Here's where you ask applicants
to put their money where their
mouse is. Sitzer recommends
starting off by sending applicants an interactive "e-roleplay"
scenario online to assess how
they respond to a challenging
customer email inquiry. Be sure
that the e-roleplay you create
reflects the types of inquiries
your center typically receives;
i.e., sales-related, service-related,
etc. When evaluating responses,
take note of whether or not the
applicant correctly interpreted
the inquiry, provided a concise,
well-written response and de-
monstrated other appropriate
skills (i.e., upselling, personaliza-
tion). Also, check to see that he
or she is familiar with the rules of "netiquette."

Is There a Shortage of Multimedia Talent?

In a 2001 study by Initiatives Three
Inc., a consulting firm specializing in
phone and Web initiatives to improve
customer support, nearly all call center
participants indicated that the desired
traits for Net reps differ from those of
phone agents. However, only 33 percent
of participants whose centers handle
email and Web transactions have a formal
Net rep recruiting and hiring process in
place.

So is it true that there is such a shortage of agents with the skills necessary to
work in today's multimedia call center?
Or is it that today's multimedia call centers aren't looking in the right places or
screening for the right skill sets? With so
many college graduates who have grown
up in the age of the Internet and text-
based communication, it's hard to believe
that the former is the case.

If your center handles Web-chat transactions, schedule a chat-based interview
with applicants. This will enable you to learn more about each candidate while evaluating their real-time, interactive writing skills. In addition to the interview, call centers such as Goodwill Toronto conduct chat-based e-roleplays to see how candidates
respond to a live customer support transaction online.

"I play the customer and give [applicants] a situation," explains Sharon Myatt, director of program development and innovation at Goodwill Toronto. "Here I test the skills they need to succeed in chat: grammar, keyboarding, critical thinking, paraphrasing and questioning."

Don't forget to assess Net rep applicants' ability to handle voice-based customer transactions via a telephone interview. This is important even if your Net reps aren't responsible for handling VoIP contacts and/or Web callbacks. Why? The phone is still the primary mode of contact in most call centers, thus having Net reps who can help out on the phones when necessary is an added bonus.

• **Conduct face-to-face interviews.** Once you've found candidates who have the core Net rep skills you're seeking, invite them into the call center. This gives each applicant a chance to see the center and gives you a chance to evaluate his interpersonal skills.

"There's more to being a Net rep than managing and establishing online relationships," Sitzer explains. "Online agents will also need to integrate successfully with your entire operation. That means responding to coaching and working well with peers. Face-to-face interviews ensure that your top choices can thrive in your dynamic environment."

Don't Forget the Phones

While email and Web-based transactions are certainly increasing in most call centers, the phone is still — and will likely remain to be — the primary mode of customer contact. As a manager of a multimedia operation, remember it's important not to get so caught up in the search for Net reps that you forget your need for dedicated phone staff. Finding Net reps who can effectively handle online as well as phone transactions can be very difficult. Therefore, you will likely need to have a separate recruiting program in place to acquire quality phone agents.

Considering the exorbitant demand for skilled phone staff in our industry, relying solely on traditional recruiting methods isn't sufficient for finding and assessing quality candidates. While newspaper ads and references from existing agents can be effective, progressive call center managers incorporate some of the following recruiting and assessment techniques into their hiring programs.

• **Partnerships with local educational institutions.** Numerous colleges, universities and trade schools have added special call center/customer service certificate programs to their curriculum. Forming alliances with such institutions can provide you with a continuous supply of qualified staff who are serious about call center careers. These schools are always looking for call center partners that can help out with course development and provide students with agent internships during the academic year. In return, the schools give the call centers first crack at new graduates.

• **Internet job postings and Interactive Voice Recognition (IVR) applicant screening.** The Web isn't just useful for attracting Net reps. Most serious job seekers spend the majority of their time on the Internet today, as they are allured by the speed in which they can find jobs opportunities and respond online. Thus posting phone agent openings on your Web site, online career centers and call center-specific Web sites is a wise strategy. Ask all phone agent applicants to email their resume and cover letter, but don't use the Web for screening purposes with these candidates. You are looking for phone agents, not email and chat experts, so why not use the phone channel as an initial screening device? This can be done quickly and effectively via the call center IVR system, says Anne Nickerson, editor and publisher of the "Call Center Insider" electronic newsletter.

"Screening applicants via the IVR is one of the biggest time-savers for human resource and call center managers," says Nickerson. "You determine the minimum qualifications you are looking for — what you would usually peruse in a stack of resumes — and, instead, ask those questions with voice or keypad responses." She adds that the IVR system can be programmed to rank top candidates based on their responses. (Several vendors provide IVR profiling services; check out www.Wonderlic.com or www.iiserve.com.)

• **IVR job postings.** The IVR unit is not only ideal for screening applicants, it's a cost-effective tool for advertising job openings. Your call center receives thousands of calls each day. Many of your customers may be in the job market or know of somebody who is. Many call centers have found that a simple announcement in the IVR greeting can be a more efficient recruiting method than placing an ad in the

Chapter 2

local paper (i.e., "Press '5' for job opportunities"). Callers who choose this option can then be immediately routed to the automated applicant screening system described previously.

As with Net rep applicants, further assessment of phone agent applicants' skills is best done via interviews and role-plays. The difference is that these assessment methods should be voice-based, not text-based, from the start. Conduct phone interviews with quality applicants to better assess their phone voices and personalities. Here's your chance to ask more detailed questions than were asked during the IVR screening process. Be sure to present applicants with a challenging customer situation and ask them how they would handle it. Do the applicant's responses sound genuine or do they seem scripted — lacking thought and creativity? Does he or she sound confident, friendly and professional? Is humor used appropriately?

Invite candidates who fare well during the phone interview in for a face-to-face interview. Conduct realistic customer role-plays, with the applicant seated at a computer. Take note of his or her customer support/sales skills, as well as his or her ability to quickly and accurately fill in basic customer information screens.

Revamped but Realistic Recruiting

In today's multimedia call center environment, you can't expect all agents to be all things to all customers all the time. However, you can develop strategic recruiting strategies to ensure that all customer contacts — whether via email, Web or phone — are handled by skilled agents all the time.

The quest for universal agents — those who can effectively handle any transaction type — is a noble one, but don't expect a high percentage of your staff to fill such oversized shoes. Online customer support is quite a different animal than traditional phone support, and there's nothing wrong with using separate teams to tame the two beasts.

However, there is something wrong with clinging to yesterday's staid hiring methods to find staff who can manage today's multichannel mix. The Web-savvy staff you need exists, you just need to peek around a few new corners when recruiting.

Call Center Managers Turn to Employment Specialists for Staffing Solutions

by Leslie Hansen Harps

Rather than tackle the recruitment and selection of agents themselves when starting up a new call center in Boise, Idaho, a year and a half ago, MCI WorldCom immediately began working with KellyConnect, a unit of Kelly Services that specializes in call center staffing. According to call center manager Alan Aikman, this move freed his staff and management team to focus on managing the call center.

"We're an outsourcing center for Hewlett-Packard" Aikman continues. "HP has a great reputation and a high-quality product; and they're very concerned with the services they receive. Working with KellyConnect allowed us the time to work closely with HP, to make sure we set center goals and that we are providing the level of support required by the customer."

The need to leverage management time, a shrinking labor pool, low unemployment rates and a sharp growth in the number of call centers are increasingly driving call center managers like Aikman to turn to employment agencies and staffing companies for the qualified, motivated personnel they need to staff their call centers.

"[Call centers] need a service such as ours," reports Delza Neblett, vice president of the Caller Access Division of Remedy Intelligent Staffing in Aliso Viejo, California. "Markets are over-employed, so good candidates are hard to come by."

Agencies Renew Call Center Focus

In the past, general employment agencies did not always do a great job at matching candidates with the client company or the call center environment in general. Research that Remedy conducted, for example, indicated that call center managers felt that "staffing companies in general didn't know what call centers did, didn't understand the pressures on an agent, nor the multitasking ability an agent needed to have," according to Neblett.

Traditional staffing companies may have used skills-based testing to measure a candidate's word processing and computer skills, but often did not conduct the behavioral tests that would identify individuals who were well suited to the call center environment and who had the necessary communication, problem-solving and decision-making skills.

"We had to look at our human performance technology — the way we look at 'can do' and 'will do' skills — a little differently," Neblett says, "and to focus on soft skills as well as hard skills."

To respond more effectively to the specific needs of call centers, employment agencies like Remedy have established divisions that specialize in call center staffing. Many of these companies have developed unique tools to find and recruit agents who are suited to the call center and, where appropriate, to temporary work. The result: higher retention and productivity as well as lower turnover and costs at client call centers.

A Wide Range of Staffing Options

Leading staffing companies, including Kelly Services, Manpower, Olsten Staffing and Remedy Intelligent Staffing, offer a wide range of options to meet call center staffing needs. Managers can use one or a combination of the following staffing approaches:

Temporary. Temporary agents may be used to fill staffing gaps during peaks in the call center on a regular basis, or to handle special projects (such as a new product introduction). Seasonal assignments (i.e., handling heavy volume during the holiday season) may have a firm beginning and end. Other, more long-term assignments may be open-ended, with temporary workers supplementing a core group of permanent agents on the call center's staff.

Temporary to permanent. This increasingly popular approach has two key benefits: first, the call center can try out a potential employee on the job before making the decision to hire. Second, since the likelihood of turnover is generally highest during an agent's first three or four months on the job, the temp-to-perm approach helps companies minimize their investment in agents who wind up leaving.

For example, MCI WorldCom brings in agents on a temporary-to-permanent basis for 90 days. When giving the three-month performance review of a temporary worker — who remains on Kelly Services' payroll — a supervisor decides whether or not to convert the agent to a full-time staffer, according to Aikman. Agents who are hired by MCI WorldCom receive benefits after successfully completing an additional three-month period.

Permanent. Sometimes called "direct placement," this is the more traditional approach to staffing, wherein the staffing agency identifies candidates, prescreens them, then presents them to the call center (or the company's human resources department) for selection. These employees immediately go on the call center's payroll.

In addition, some staffing companies offer on-site management to oversee temporary or contingent agents or to manage the entire operation. But companies that have had call centers for years have recruited and hired their own call center agents. Why are they now willing to pay an employment agency to do the job? In part because staffing is the core competency of employment agencies, thus they can afford to make the investment required in areas such as:

- Research that reveals the behavior, skills and attributes of successful call center agents.
- Development of specialized testing instruments that identify candidates most likely to perform well in the call center.
- A wide range of recruitment approaches that enable them to assemble a large pool of skilled workers.
- Training specifically targeted to the call center environment.

Revving Up Recruiting

Several staffing agencies that specialize in call centers have invested heavily in understanding what type of person does best in the call center — and where to find them.

For example, when developing its KellyConnect call center solution, Kelly Services created a strategic recruiting program that is built on an extensive candidate

Chapter 2

profiling system. Explains Teresa Setting, director of product management and recruiting for the company, "We took all of the individuals who worked in call centers for Kelly for the past year and matched their names and addresses against a consumer segmentation database." This enabled the company to identify the "demographics, geographics and psychographics" of the agents, including their interests, likes and dislikes, age ranges, activities, where they're located, etc. Such information enables KellyConnect to successfully locate candidates with similar characteristics.

KellyConnect uses a national advertising agency to buy television and radio advertising, which can result in substantial economies of scale. Manpower has a whole range of recruiting techniques it uses, some of which are more effective in certain markets than in others. "We have about 10 different ways to go after employees," says Linda Lauritzen, director of global call center services for Manpower in Milwaukee. One of the most effective is through referrals from the company's existing employee base. In addition, the staffing companies are increasingly using the Internet for recruiting purposes. For example, Kelly Services' online Kelly Career Network gives potential candidates 24-hour access to job postings. Applicants can select their preferences for work from 30 categories, including call center positions. The system searches job openings and notifies the branch that posted the open job. The branch then contacts the candidate for followup.

Like the other employment agencies, Remedy has a pool of qualified candidates from which to draw, some of whom are prequalified to work in certain areas such as customer care or sales.

At Olsten Staffing Services, "we are always actively recruiting people, whether for call centers or secretarial or technical positions. It's what we do, our core business," explains Linda Gherardi, director of teleservices product development for the Melville, New York, company.

Testing Aptitude and Attitude

Olsten starts its selection process with a telephone prescreen of prospects, reports Gherardi. "If they're a good candidate for the call center, we bring them in for a personal behavioral interview," she says, plus a "real world" job preview specific to a client's location. Where possible, this preview is done on the customer site, which enables the candidate to get a firsthand look at the work environment.

As part of its evaluation process, Olsten uses a proprietary system that evaluates candidates' competency in software and data entry. In addition, the company uses "Selection Advantage," a CD-ROM program from Kaplan Learning Centers that tests customer service skills, including soft skills (such as interpersonal styles, establishing rapport, making sure needs are met), investigative skills, problem-solving and speed, including multitasking. "Candidates listen to a series of 25 calls, then choose the best response from four or five possible responses," according to Gherardi.

In addition, she says, Olsten is finding that the ability to respond to customer email is increasingly important, so the company is testing for business-writing skills and spelling, as appropriate.

KellyConnect uses a battery of behavioral assessment tools to determine whether the individual is suited for the job. "In call centers, 80 percent of performance is behavior rather than hard skills," Setting explains.

Manpower uses validated proprietary tools that measure phone skills and voice quality, as well as assesses a candidate's behavioral attributes and abilities. Manpower, like other companies, may conduct a job analysis to identify the critical skills and skill levels for a particular call center, and can also develop a "success profile" for a particular site.

Targeted Training

"There's a huge shortage of staff in the marketplace with call center skills," observes Manpower's Lauritzen. To expand the pool of skilled workers, employment agencies have partnered with training providers or have developed their own training.

For example, Manpower has created three call center training programs as part of the company's SkillWare training, which is designed to equip its employees with skills that are in high demand in the marketplace.

KellyConnect recently partnered with a training company, which will provide interactive multimedia training to call center agents. Included will be inbound and outbound training plus a module on effective leadership, according to Dina O'Mara, product manager of call center staffing. In addition, a separate module focuses on the collections environment.

"We provide basic-level skills training so that, when employees are brought onto the assignment, they can focus on the client's training. This makes the client's training more time-efficient."

"Temporary" Staffing Challenges

Temporary agents — whether short-term, supplemental, seasonal or temp-to-perm — can provide crucial flexibility for call centers. And "temping" has become a way of life for some staffers, who also like the flexibility it offers.

But there are challenges to staffing with temp workers. For example, AutoNation — the world's largest auto retailer — uses temporary workers from Olsten Staffing in its benefits group. Many of these agents seek permanent, full-time work, but AutoNation has limited permanent positions. "While we've converted some temporary workers to full-time, even more want to convert to full-time and, right now, that's not our staffing model," explains to Cynthia Boudreaux, business lead for benefits administration and quality for AutoNation.

Managing a blended workforce made up of permanent and temporary staff requires special care. According to Manpower's Linda Lauritzen, "In a call center, it's particularly important that our employees feel the same level of value for their services as our customer's employees." Problems can occur when temp workers feel that their contributions are appreciated less than that of their permanent peers. "There can't be a dichotomy in the way you treat them," says Lauritzen, who recommends that its call center clients include temp agents in meetings and, when possible, involve them in joint projects with full-time staff.

Finding the Right Vendor

Not all employment agencies specialize in call center staffing. To make sure that you're working with a company that understands your needs, Remedy's Neblitt suggests that you ask the following questions:

- Does the agency truly understand call centers?
- Is the agency willing and able to do a specific needs assessment for your operation?
- What kind of investment have they made to ensure that they recruit the right people?
- Do they use recruitment and selection tools developed specifically for the call center environment?
- What assistance is the company willing to provide? For example, will the company provide its clients with market surveys?
- Do they have a good on-site program (putting managers on site to supervise temporary workers) if that is the right solution?

Asking such questions can help you find the right staffing agency that will partner with you to recruit, hire and keep good people. The effort can pay off in increased retention, with some companies reporting a 30 percent to 40 percent reduction in turnover, thanks to improved screening and hiring practices. According to AutoNation's Boudreaux, "It has been extremely worthwhile — we're running at under 10 percent on typical turnover for temporary workers."

Visit these Web sites for more information:

www.kellyservices.com

www.manpower.com

www.olsten.com

www.remedystaff.com

Chapter 2

ETS Strikes It Rich
Tapping Contract Worker Pool

by Greg Levin

The Educational Testing Service (ETS) call center in Princeton, New Jersey, is achieving its own high scores using contract employees to improve customer service by 33 percent while saving $8 million a year. Two-thirds of the ETS 550 phone reps are temporary. They work contractually during the ETS busy season, which begins each year in September and ends in June. The center handles questions about national standardized aptitude tests, such as the Scholastic Assessment Test (SAT) and the Graduate Records Exam (GRE), from 8 a.m. until 10 p.m. weekdays.

"There's a dramatic increase in our call volume during the academic year," says Louis DeLauro, executive director of ETS, "so the ability to expand and contract our staff capacity is attractive to us. With contract employees, we are able not only to meet our call peaks, we are able to save money during the valleys when we need only our full-time reps on the phones." The ETS average of 10,000 calls a week during the summer climbs to about 62,000 calls a week during the academic year.

Without the contract workers, who are obtained through local employment agencies, ETS would need to maintain a large full-time staff, half of whom would have little or nothing to do during the slow times, but who would still need to be paid and receive benefits. "The $8 million a year isn't really a savings, it's a cost-avoidance," says DeLauro. "That's how much we would have to pay if all of our employees were full time. And keeping our costs down enables us to keep the price of tests down for all the kids."

Raising Quality of Core Staff and Customer Service

Using agency personnel also gives ETS a ready way to "try out" potential full-time call center employees — before hiring them.

"Many members of our regular staff started out as contract workers," DeLauro says. "We can see who among the agency staff are the high performers, the 'cream of the crop.' It's an outstanding way for us to acquire an excellent core group of regular, full-time employees. It also has led to a low turnover rate among our full-time staff because the reps we choose have already worked in the position for some time and know what the job entails."

Maintaining such a strong team of full-time reps over the years has led to a significant increase in customer satisfaction, according to the ETS annual customer satisfaction survey. The initial survey, conducted in the early 1980s, indicated a customer satisfaction rating of only 58 percent. As ETS began using contract workers and improved training in the mid-1980s, survey ratings began to improve dramatically.

"As we've culled out the top-performers among the agency staff and added them to our full-time staff, ratings have gone up," says DeLauro. "Today, our average customer satisfaction rating is 91 percent."

Smooth Transition and Careful Selection Behind Success

The transition to a contract worker-based staff has been a smooth one. When ETS began using contract employees 10 years ago, they made up less than 10 percent of the total staff. "We gradually increased that number over the years as full-time employees have left and as the business has grown," explains DeLauro. "We haven't had any involuntary displacement of regular staff."

ETS agency personnel range from young men and women just out of high school to retirees. To ensure that the people sent by the various employment agencies are qualified to handle call center work, ETS interviews and later calls candidates to hear how they sound on the phone. "We don't take just anybody that an agency sends," explains Betty Wargo, ETS customer service manager, "We want to make sure not only that they are right for us, but that we are right for them."

Aspiring to become a member of the regular staff is not a requirement for being hired as a contract worker. "Not every rep who comes from an agency wants to become a full-time staff member," says Wargo. "A lot of our agency staff are college students, retirees or mothers, and they like having the time off during the summer." In addition to phone staff, ETS employs a number of temporary "noninquiry" personnel who handle a variety of nonphone tasks, such as customer correspondence.

High Turnover, Continuous Training Among Challenges

The use of contract workers at ETS is not without challenges, the biggest of which is high turnover of temporary staff.

"Once we let the agency staff go for July and August," explains DeLauro, "they often end up temping or finding full-time jobs at other organizations and don't return in the fall."

Only about 25 percent of the agency staff who have their contracts renewed return for the following academic year. ETS is working to reduce turnover by providing its contract labor with attractive incentives, such as cash bonuses.

The high turnover leads to another challenge. "We are constantly retraining," says DeLauro. "We need to train at least a couple hundred workers at the beginning of every academic year."

Nonetheless, the benefits of employing contract workers far outweigh the drawbacks, DeLauro says. "With all of the positive benefits resulting from using contract employees, we can live with the few negative things."

Although the continuous training of new agency personnel is time-consuming, ETS doesn't skimp on quality in that area. Contract workers receive the same training as regular staff. Each trainee receives from two to 10 days of specific training on the program for which he or she will handle calls. Following these program-specific sessions, trainees receive two days of general customer service training, which includes discussions on appropriate greetings, probing, providing empathy and closing, as well as dealing with irate customers. Before going on the phones, all trainees participate in role-plays that simulate typical customer calls.

Like One of the Family

Agency staff are treated like permanent workers, earning pay raises for improved performance and participating in team projects and company outings.

Such equity is a primary reason for ETS success with using contract workers, says manager Wargo.

"Everybody here is treated the same," she says. "In fact, we surveyed the contract

Chapter 2

workers a few years ago to find out how they felt about working here, and they all said that they were treated just as well as the regular staff.

"The agency personnel aren't taken for granted," Wargo continues. "We don't just use them when we need them and then coldly cast them away. If they do a good job, agency personnel have the potential for a great future here."

Jane Borden, an ETS team leader, can attest to that. "I started out as an agency worker over five years ago," recalls Borden. "Within six months, I was offered a full-time position. I gladly accepted and today I am a team leader."

Borden helps supervise and coach reps, and says she hears a lot of positive comments from contract employees about how they are treated at ETS.

"Many of the agency staff have said that this job is so unlike any other agency job that they've had," she says. "At most other companies, they were only expected to work for a week. They say that they simply did what they needed to do to get through that week. However, at ETS, they say they feel like a part of the company."

Creating a Deeper Pool

With the potential for improving company, customer and employee satisfaction, DeLauro is surprised that more call centers are not using contract workers.

"Employment agencies can provide flexible human resource options. I don't know why more customer service centers don't utilize them," he says. "While many companies do use agency staff for things like telemarketing or for some order fulfillment tasks, few use them in a true customer service environment. If more organizations started using agency staff in the call center, agencies would begin to develop a large pool of experienced customer service workers. Having access to such workers would help call centers shorten training times and provide them with high-caliber reps for hiring."

College Call Center Programs Help to Fill Shallow Labor Pool

by Greg Levin

Call center work is not for "just anybody," but with industry growth soaring and competition for qualified staff tightening, many call centers managers say they have had to hire "just anybody" to handle their ever-increasing call volume.

"Finding qualified staff for our call center is extremely difficult," says Michelle Ingersoll, staffing leader for American Express Financial Advisors in Minneapolis. "There are a lot of companies seeking the same types of employees as we are, so when it comes to interviewing for agent positions in the call center, I find that the pickings are somewhat slim."

Many managers who share Ingersoll's predicament are going back to school — not to take classes themselves, but to find qualified agents for their call centers. A host of colleges and other postsecondary educational institutions in the United States and Canada have created formal call center programs in response to the recent industry boom. Many of these programs are relatively new. Some that have been around for several years are just now capturing attention as the call center labor pool becomes shallower and shallower, particularly in larger cities.

"Our program provides a solution to a very real problem; call centers in our area need highly skilled people to fill customer contact positions," says Dan Lowe, program manager for the Customer Contact Training Program offered at Kirkwood Community College in Cedar Rapids, Iowa. "There are a lot of people in the area who, given the training, can become highly effective call center reps. We are increasing the pool of qualified candidates for these positions."

Bob Davis, national customer service manager for Toyota Financial Services in Cedar Rapids, looks forward to recruiting agents from Kirkwood Community College's new program. "The customer service center training [program] will allow us to [fill] our applicant pool with qualified and quality associates for our organization," he says.

No single college call center program can produce enough skilled agents for every call center in its region. But such programs — with more in the planning stages throughout North America — are already easing many call centers' recruiting and training woes.

"We've hired a few agents who've graduated from the call center training program at the College de l'Outaouais," says Ann Lapalice, manager of the Canadian Medical Protection Association's call center in Ottawa, Ontario. "We like to hire these graduates because they're already trained on computer applications, telephone etiquette, etc. They're ready to take on the job of call center agent." The College de l'Outaouais is one of six colleges in Quebec that offer the 765-hour Call Centre Agent Training Program.

Call Centers Take Active Role in Program Development

Most of today's college call center training programs were created in direct response to local companies speaking out about their need for skilled agents. "We decided to create our training program after talking with a number of businesses that either had a call center, or were planning a call center, in the Dallas area, and that were seeking a large base of skilled employees," explains Bob Arnold, senior training consultant for the Bill Priest Institute (BPI) — the workforce training unit of the Dallas County Community College District. BPI's 480-hour Call Center/Customer Service program is expected to train more than 500 people for entry-level call center jobs before the end of this year.

Dan Lowe tells a similar story regarding the start-up of Kirkwood Community College's program in Cedar Rapids. "Our entire program was the result of area businesses approaching us about their need for more highly skilled call center representatives."

Germana Community College in Fredericksburg, Virginia, developed its 19-credit hour Call Center Career Studies program in response to a single company's request. "GEICO Insurance came to us and asked if we could create a program to help enhance the call center labor pool in the area," recalls Dr. Kay Dunkley, director of the Center for Workforce and Community Excellence at Germana Community College. "They were struggling to employ skilled workers." Today,

GEICO and several other companies with call centers in the area work closely with the school's program.

A few of today's programs in the United States got a big financial boost from state grants. For example, Kirkwood Community College received $556,000 from the Iowa Department of Economic Development to develop and deliver its program. BPI was awarded a $1.02 million Skills Development Fund grant from the Texas Workforce Commission. Programs that have not received grants are funded primarily by the school itself and donations from area businesses that stand to benefit from an enhanced labor pool.

In most cases, the colleges and the local call centers have collaborated in developing the program curriculum, which typically includes classes on key call center concepts, customer service, phone skills, sales skills, computer skills, business math and English, as well as general "workplace readiness" training. Courses are usually taught by certified instructors who have been trained on the specific curriculum and who have a customer service/call center background or general business background. In a few cases, local call center professionals help teach classes.

Hands-On Experience a Key Part of Programs

Today's existing college call center agent programs feature not only intensive classroom instruction (up to 615 hours in some programs), but ample hands-on experience via in-depth call simulation exercises and/or student internships at local call centers. A few programs even have their own call center lab on campus where students in the latter stages of training can gain invaluable experience. BPI, for example, sends all students who complete the program's course-work to its simulated call center, equipped with 25 PC workstations. Here, students take part in extensive role-plays where they follow scripted call scenarios provided by the program's call center sponsors.

Such hands-on experience is essential in preparing students for the rigors of call center work, says Marty Tally of GTE, one of BPI's program sponsors. "The students leave with a realistic review of what the call center environment is all about," she explains. "Those who choose to take jobs as agents do so knowing exactly what is expected of them from the onset, and thus are less likely to leave after just a few months."

Pretrained Agents = Serious Savings

Call centers that partner with local colleges offering call center agent programs can potentially save significantly on recruiting and training costs. Most schools give supporting call centers first pick of new program graduates, often eliminating the need for the centers to pay for classified ads when seeking new agents. And because the graduates are fresh out of an in-depth call center training program, the time — and money — required to train them to handle calls may be greatly reduced. Often all that is needed is a week or so of focused training on the company's specific products/services and procedures.

Tom Thomas, a Phoenix-based call center consultant and proponent of call center college education, recently conducted a study that revealed the potential savings in training time that can be realized by call centers tapping into college programs. Thomas' consulting firm — Thomas & Associates — surveyed numerous call centers in the greater Phoenix area and found that roughly two-thirds of the major training areas covered during new-hire training at most centers could easily be taught in external programs. Of the key training areas listed by study respondents — company business, PCs and software, customer service, internal systems, problem-solving, and time management — only company business and internal systems would require specific training by the call center itself. "A big chunk of the rest of the key training areas are already covered by most [college programs], saving call centers a lot of time and training dollars," says Thomas.

Programs Promoting Careers, Not Just Jobs

Perhaps as important as the extensive training these programs provide is the focus on promoting call center careers, not just jobs. Simply churning out a new crop of semitrained bodies to fill empty seats at local centers is not the intention of today's successful college call center programs. Instead, these programs educate students on the importance and value of call center work, and promote the opportunities in this rapidly growing field. "We strive to set up students for successful careers, not only as agents, but perhaps later on as supervisors or managers," says Rena Posteraro, coordinator of Call Centre Training at Niagara College in Welland, Ontario. Such an approach inspires graduates to perform, fosters pride in workmanship and leads to reduced turnover once on the job, she says.

It's difficult to find that level of agent enthusiasm and confidence when hiring agents "off the street," says Kirkwood's Lowe. Most respondents to call center help-wanted ads lack significant experience in and knowledge of the unique call center environment, he explains. While it is up to the center itself to select and train the most promising applicants, time is usually not on the center's side due to staffing pressures. As a result, the call center often rushes through the hiring and training process and pushes new-hires onto the phones. These agents typically don't fully understand their roles and feel overwhelmed by the pace of work. The result: low morale and high attrition.

Using Education to Attract New Call Centers

College agent programs do more than create career opportunities for the unemployed/underemployed and supply existing call centers with much-needed skilled staff. With the help of strong marketing efforts led by economic development agencies and other entities, these programs are capturing the attention of businesses seeking new call center sites. For instance, BPI works with the Greater Dallas Chamber of Commerce to encourage companies to move their call center operations to Dallas, using the agent training program as a major incentive.

Some cities/regions are building entire economic revival plans around their call center initiatives. "We were given a mandate by the government of Quebec to attract American and European companies to establish call centers to the region to bolster our economy," explains Brigitte Simard, vice president of sales and marketing for Vision Quebec, a firm dedicated to the promotion of Quebec as an "ideal location" for call centers.

These programs are an excellent start, but they're not a silver bullet. With economic development specialists aggressively marketing regions as call center "havens"

Chapter 2

with educational programs in place, the familiar problem of "not enough agents to go around" is a concern. The pressure on college programs to continually fill the pool with skilled agents to meet the growing call center population's needs can be significant. Programs that produce 50 graduates several times a year will not meet the surging demand for more agents in most regions.

Colleges and economic development agencies need to work together not only to attract new students, but also to set realistic goals about the number of graduates the programs can produce and to clearly communicate those goals to the local call center community.

More Colleges Catching Call Center Craze

With call center growth continuing at a rapid pace (the Gartner Group estimates growth at 20 percent per year), you can expect more college call center programs to pop up in the near future. Numerous community colleges and universities are currently in the planning stages, says consultant Thomas.

"I was invited to speak at the American Association of Community Colleges' annual meeting to discuss the opportunities in call center education. Many in the audience were very interested in this topic and are looking into how they can create training programs at their colleges."

Several institutions that currently offer call center programs are sharing their knowledge with interested parties. "There are a couple of other community colleges in Virginia that are planning to use our program as a model in developing their own curriculum," says Dr. Dunkley of Germana Community College.

As a call center professional, it might be wise to start forming alliances with local postsecondary schools now to ensure that your skilled agent pool doesn't run dry.

Chapter 3:
Selecting the Right Candidates

CIGNA Uses Computerized Applicant-Screening System to Identify Top Agent Candidates

by Julia Mayben

Although CIGNA HealthCare knows that it's the people in the call center who determine its success, it has turned to technology to help find them. When CIGNA revamped its hiring procedures at its two largest call centers in July 1997, the company implemented a computerized applicant-screening program, called JASS (Job Applicant Screening System). Less than a year later, CIGNA is seeing significant results in terms of reduced turnover and increased cost savings.

"We wanted to improve how applicants are screened and selected," says Eileen Sylvester, who as project manager for call center consulting at CIGNA developed the hiring pilot at the two call centers. "JASS has helped us shorten the interview process and hire better candidates who have a more realistic idea of what the job entails. [As a result], we've reduced rep turnover during training by 40 percent and predict cost savings of 300 percent per new-hire."

JASS is a customized, interactive software program that screens and rates applicants automatically. It provides a simulated work environment, including customer phone calls, to measure key customer service competencies like listening ability, computer literacy, problem-solving and typing skills. The JASS system was originally developed by Purdue University in conjunction with Multimedia Magic, and is now owned by E-Talk Corporation. Companies that purchase the basic JASS system customize it to meet the specific hiring needs of their call center operations.

Weeding Out Rep "Wannabees"

CIGNA HealthCare uses JASS in the initial phase of its new three-pronged hiring process at its call centers in Charlotte, North Carolina, and Phoenix. The system's sole purpose is to determine early on if applicants have the basic skills to succeed in the call center environment. Applicants whose skills are rated acceptable by

JASS take a written "service aptitude" test. Those who pass the written test are invited in for a personal interview.

All new applicants complete the JASS computerized test in CIGNA's human resources department. The program takes anywhere from 90 minutes to three hours to complete, depending on the applicant. "When applicants come in, we direct them to the room with the computer setups and headsets. They work at their own speed, except during the call simulations because those are timed," explains Sylvester.

CIGNA's application of the JASS system consists of several components. The first two are designed to acquaint applicants with the company. These sections feature brief audio and visual overviews of CIGNA. Applicants then watch a 10-minute video that Sylvester calls a "realistic job preview for applicants." The video includes existing CIGNA reps talking about what it's like to work in the call center. It also explains the basic job requirements, such as good communication skills, computer literacy, customer service experience/potential and promptness.

JASS then takes applicants through a complete online job application, which is transferred automatically to the human resources department. The next screenpop schedules interview times. Applicants are asked for three possible times in one week when they could return for an in-person interview. "By automating these two tasks, we save time," says Martine Maness, human resources manager at the CIGNA HealthCare call center in Charlotte.

Next is a tutorial on how to handle the upcoming simulated phone calls. "We give applicants information on things like how to work on the screen and where to find information," says Maness. "It's very detailed, so all applicants are on the same playing field."

JASS' final component consists of eight audio customer call simulations in which applicants listen via a headset and respond to "callers" by selecting answers from four choices that appear on their computer screen. Several questions are asked during each call. Applicants are also asked to type in information, such as callers' names and addresses.

All calls are generic and require no healthcare knowledge. "Healthcare is something we can train; we want to determine what skills they have," says Sylvester. The recorded calls used in the simulations feature both male and female callers who range from pleasant to angry. One example of an upset caller is a woman who calls to complain about a cleaning solution that didn't remove a stain out of her carpet. The questions applicants must answer in this scenario involve how they would handle the frustrated caller, who misused the cleaning product.

Once they complete the computerized test, applicants are either instructed to leave or to wait in a conference room while the results are tabulated, depending on how busy the human resources department is. Applicants are graded on a "pass/fail" system. To determine the minimum passing grade, CIGNA HealthCare enlisted a statistician to conduct validity studies, using information from existing reps. Based on that information, the company selected scoring guidelines for JASS.

The computerized testing, though extensive and sometimes exhausting, hasn't deterred applicants. In fact, no one has walked out of a JASS test yet at either of the two centers. "We give them an introduction before we get started to try to eliminate any intimidation," explains Maness. She adds that leaving applicants on their own helps overcome intimidation, too. "They can pick up the phone or walk around the corner to our offices if they need us. From what we've seen, they like to take the test themselves and not have the stress of someone looking over their shoulder."

Overall Hiring Process Streamlined

Applicants aren't the only ones who like the self-directed aspect of computerized testing. Managers appreciate the time that JASS has freed up for them. "You don't need anyone there taping calls or doing the evaluations," says Sylvester. "The computer does all the calculations and prints out the final score. That saves us time and money."

Maness agrees. "We've been able to cut the recruiting time significantly," she says. Now, we have more time to devote to interviewing candidates who have been effectively prescreened."

In the past, CIGNA HealthCare's hiring process required managers to spend up to 12 hours a day screening and evaluating applicants over the phone. Not only was this time consuming, it provided much less in-depth information about candidates' skills than JASS does. After the phone interviews, qualified applicants were invited into the call center for a skills assessment test. Here, they took "live" calls, which were actually calls initiated by a human resources representative posing as a customer. Two other managers taped the calls, and later reviewed and evaluated them. Those evaluations determined whether or not applicants were asked back for live interviews.

Today, the skills assessment portion of the hiring process involves just a quick written test because applicants who make it to that level have already had their basic call-handling skills tested by JASS. And, while live interviews are still part of the overall hiring process, they are less time-consuming because only well-qualified applicants make it through the screening.

While JASS has been successful for CIGNA, Sylvester reminds managers of other call centers that the system involves more than just "plug and play." Before a company can enjoy the benefits JASS can provide, it has to tailor the system to meets its specific hiring needs. As Sylvester explains, "The basic JASS system includes tutorials and generic call simulations. You need to customize the video portions to enhance the entire process."

Sylvester acknowledges that CIGNA's customization experience was taxing. "We had to do a lot of research," she recalls. "We also had to spend time creating the background information and presenting it in the right way."

The initial efforts paid off. "We didn't have any kinks to work through when we started using JASS with applicants because by the time we had it in place, it had been tested and retested," recalls Maness.

Long-Term Turnover Tale Yet to Be Told

Although the new hiring program has enabled CIGNA HealthCare to cut rep turnover during training by nearly half at the two centers, it's too soon to tell what impact it will have on rep turnover over the longer haul. Still, Maness is confident they will be able to reduce rep turnover after training, too. She believes reps will want to stay at the centers because "JASS has helped us hire people who are better suited to the job. With JASS, we get to know them better and they get to know us. They get a taste of what the job will be like."

Now that computerized applicant screening has been deemed a success, CIGNA plans to roll it out to its other call centers later this spring. "It has met all the goals we set out to accomplish," says Sylvester. "We'd like to see the same benefits at the other call centers."

Specialized Pre-Employment Screening Pays Off for Call Centers

by Greg Levin

After discovering that their current hiring methods were providing unsatisfactory results, call center managers at Blue Cross and Blue Shield (BCBS) of Alabama began reviewing new staff-selection practices.

"We had hired some people who, after six months on the phones, weren't as effective and productive as we had anticipated when we hired them," recalls Susan Palmer, call center manager of BCBS of Alabama, located in Birmingham.

Call centers have struggled with high turnover for years. Some phone reps quit because they are unhappy with the job itself, or with the incentives, training or management style at their call center. Others are let go because of insufficient skills, reliability or motivation. Regardless of whether reps quit or are terminated, high turnover rates are a signal that a call center should take a second look at the way it selects its staff.

That's just what the managers at BCBS of Alabama did.

"We looked at some of our veteran phone reps who we thought had been very successful," says Palmer, "and tried to pinpoint the characteristics that made them successful."

They were able to identify several key characteristics, including the reps' ability to organize thoughts clearly and concisely; express empathy with their tone of voice; gain the caller's confidence; give the caller the feeling they were being treated as an important individual; and listen well.

Says Sharon Carroll-Bailey, another call center manager at the Birmingham site, "We wanted all of our reps to have these qualities, so that no matter which rep callers got, they would feel that nobody could have assisted them any better."

Finding Who Fits Through Intensive Testing, Interviewing

From their analysis, and with the help of human resources and the phone reps,

BCBS of Alabama was able to develop an effective prescreening interview process.

"Human resources reviews the resumes, looking for applicants who have had some kind of experience in customer service," explains Carroll-Bailey. "Those applicants are brought in for basic skills testing. If they pass the testing process, they are called by someone in human resources, who conducts a short telephone interview. The human resources person screens for tone of voice and ability to communicate over the phone."

Applicants who do well on the phone interview are called in for a face-to-face interview with a human resources representative. Applicants do some role-plays and learn about company policy and culture. Those who pass that screening are sent on to be interviewed by the call center managers.

"Until this point," says Carroll-Bailey, "we have not had any contact with the applicant."

A senior phone rep takes the applicant to a small conference room that is set up with an automated call distributor (ACD) and a headset. The senior rep tells the applicant the interview will be by phone, and the purpose is to hear what the customers will hear.

The applicant is then told how the ACD works. When the applicant is ready, the call center managers, who are in a separate room, call the applicant on the phone and ask him or her a set of standard questions.

"At the conclusion of this interview, " says Carroll-Bailey, "we determine whether or not we want to pursue the applicant or terminate the application process."

The managers meet with the applicants who do well on the phone interview, and plug them in with a phone rep who is taking calls.

Says Carroll-Bailey, "We tell the applicant, 'We want to give you the opportunity to see what the job is all about, what reps do on a daily basis. Please feel free to ask them any questions about the job. Then, let us know if you are interested.' So, we're actually putting the ball back in their court."

New Reps Request More Specific Training

When the call center first implemented the program, the managers asked for feedback from the people they hired using the new process.

"Most of them said they felt the interview process was very thorough," says Carroll-Bailey, "and believed they could really make it as a rep because we screened well. However, some said they didn't feel they received the training they needed after being hired to be the best rep they could be. As a result, we changed our training process."

Reps now undergo four to five weeks of classroom training where they learn about the system and the contract they will be servicing. After the classroom training, reps handle simulated calls in a "mini" call center for several weeks. Trainees take calls from senior reps and are given feedback on their performance. Reps who show proficiency in the simulated call center begin taking live calls from customers.

"Everybody Wants Our Reps!"

According to Palmer, the call center has experienced only one other problem since introducing the new hiring program. "Everybody wants our phone reps!" she says. "We have found that due to our detailed selection process, the type of people we bring into the company learn very quickly and are successful. When other areas of the company have position openings, they look to our people to fill those openings."

Of the few reps that left the call center, most now work in higher-level positions within the company. But Carroll-Bailey feels this is not a drawback, because the whole company benefits. She says since the phone reps they select are quality employees, it comes as no surprise that they are sought after by other departments. She sees it as a positive thing, a solid career path for the reps.

"We hire reps with the expectation that they will stay in the position for a minimum of 12 to 18 months," the manager explains.

Ontario Lottery Depends on More than Lady Luck to Staff Center

Ontario Lottery's call center, like BCBS of Alabama, is lowering turnover through better hiring practices.

Ontario Lottery relocated its call center to Sault Ste. Marie, Ontario, in 1992. The new center was too far from the old site, and most of the staff did not make the move. The center turned to an outside consultant to help them choose new employees who would have the best chance for success at the new call center.

Marjorie Josephs, department supervisor of the Ontario Lottery call center, says consultant Jack Green and his company, Entretel Incorporated, headquartered in Oakville, Ontario, were instrumental in getting the new center off to a strong start.

"Jack came in and learned all about our company," says Josephs. "Then he and an associate, Lynn Stevens, helped me with the hiring and training. We sat down and came up with criteria for going through resumes. We looked for things like customer service skills, computer skills and supervisory skills — we needed some people to fill shift-supervisor positions.

"Then Lynn set up a telephone interview process that was very effective. We asked the applicants general questions and paid particular attention to their tone of voice. The area we are in can be pretty high-stress, so we knew we needed people who would not lose their patience with customers."

Ontario Lottery has about 7,600 customers, from "every nationality you can think of," according to Josephs. Phone reps must have the ability to stay calm and handle calls from customers who speak very little English. "It takes a very special person to work here," she says.

After working with Green and Entretel, Josephs used the hiring skills she learned to select eight more applicants on her own. All but two of the original reps are still working at the call center.

She says she learned one essential skill for selecting quality, long-term staff.

"Being able to identify various personalities who will fit into your call center is key. Prescreening applicants and emphasizing team-building in the hiring process are also important."

Looking Beyond Good References

Consultant Green started focusing on the call center industry about three years ago. "I noticed a lot of call centers weren't very strong in the areas of hiring or training," he recalls. "I saw a lot of managers working very hard to help trainees fit into the call center, when maybe it wasn't the best job or even the best organization for the trainee in the first place."

When there's not a good fit between call center and rep, Green observes, "it's frustrating for the manager It's also frustrating for the trainee to feel failure. It's better all around, he says, if call centers can avoid or minimize turnover from the start by only hiring those employees best-suited for the call center job.

Green feels traditional hiring practices are not sufficient for effectively staffing call centers. Many companies look only at general characteristics of applicants: Do they have good references? Have they stayed at one place of work for an extended period, or have they moved from company to company? Do they have good oral and written communications skills? While these are good characteristics, Green says they are not specific enough to indicate whether or not an applicant and the call center are a match.

"We've seen many situations where a person is a good fit in one call center, but not in another. For example, somebody who may be viewed as aggressive by one company — one that doesn't emphasize individual achievement as much as team effort — may fit in very well at a company that focuses more on personal initiative.

"Another thing that complicates hiring is that many companies need to look for a balanced staff," Green says, recommending that each call center have a mix of personality types for best results. "For example, when we were helping Coca-Cola Bottling hire 35 people, we knew we didn't want 35 people who were all the same. So when we did the screening, we looked for people who we thought would be basic, solid performers, but we also looked for a few keen, 'set the world on fire,' people." Green says it works the other way as well, because if you only hire people who want to set the world on fire, you're going to be disappointed.

Problems can also occur when call centers hire only the most talented people they can find. "If the job does not require that high a level of talent, the result will be turnover," observes Green. "The employee eventually will become dissatisfied with the level of challenge."

Investing in Longevity

Managers, like those at BCBS of Alabama and Ontario Lottery, admit their new prescreening practices require a strenuous time commitment, but they know that it pays off in reduced turnover. While most call centers won't deny the benefits of intensive prescreening and interviewing, many still don't invest the necessary time and money up front to develop new hiring practices to find people who fit. These companies continue to replace and retrain workers.

Says Pam Allen, telecommunications specialist at BCBS of Alabama, "We take a lot more time than most call centers to bring people on board, but we feel that it definitely pays off down the road."

Green of Entretel agrees. "We ask our clients, 'Do you want to put your money into continually replacing and retraining people, or do you want to spend a few more dollars to help get and keep quality workers?'"

GEICO Explains Its Criteria for Hiring and Retaining Reps

by Bette Mock

Each telephone representative you hire means a major investment in time and money for your organization. You'll want to get this first step down to a science, or you'll end up with unqualified people who won't stay with your center very long. Everything else you do as a manager — forecasting calls, scheduling, queue management, budgeting, call center design — will be futile if you hire the wrong people to answer your calls.

Patrick Wilson, vice president of staff development at Government Employees Insurance Company (GEICO), designs selection systems, selection criteria and training programs for GEICO's incoming call centers in five locations across the United States. His office also trains managers in these regionalized centers to administer the selection and training procedures.

"In order to become an agent for GEICO, a lot of study, reinforcement and training is involved. Our extensive qualifying program assures that we get the right kinds of people in our call centers — those who enjoy working on the phones, those who can tolerate a fairly stressful environment with close supervision, and those who have the ability to acquire technical knowledge and make decisions for our company."

"Whether we are selecting agents for sales, claims or customer service, we use a multiple-phase program developed after a year-long study, during which we analyzed our agents' jobs. We then determined what was needed in the way of knowledge, skills and abilities to perform these jobs. A consulting firm aided in the project and, in concert with us, developed the program," he says.

"Interest Profile" — The First Hurdle

Wilson explains that the progression begins with the employment application. The applicants complete what is known as an "interest profile," a series of 45 questions that applicants score on a scale of 1 to 5, indicating "whether they would enjoy doing lots of that sort of thing, not enjoy it very much or don't care one way or the other." A battery of paper-and-pencil tests also is administered, testing abilities in reading comprehension and decision-making. This completes the first hurdle, and Wilson says that roughly 85 percent to 90 percent of applicants pass the minimal score required to continue to the next hurdle.

"Fit and Affinity"

Next, applicants are screened by a member of the human resource department. If they are found to be generally employable by GEICO, the next step is a "line interview." Here the actual supervisor over positions in that location interviews the prospective new-hire. This interview is to determine "fit and affinity" to the job. "We operate on the principle that people will enjoy doing a job and, therefore, tend to do it well and do it for long periods of time if they're using the kinds of skills and abilities that they enjoy using," says Wilson. "We get at that by determining the kinds of jobs and experiences they've had in the past, the kinds of things they enjoyed about those positions, and then relate those to the kinds of skills and abilities they need in order to perform that position.

"So it's not looking for skills and abilities — rather, it is looking for having used the skills and abilities that we know are required in our job positions." If applicants are not found qualified in "fit and affinity," they go no further in the selection process. Each hurdle must be overcome before going to the next.

"Simulation of Job"

Applicants who pass the the fit and affinity requirements, then go through a simulation exercise. They are placed on the telephone with a pair of administrators and a microcosm of the job as telephone agent takes place. This is an objective simulation with 150 opportunities to demonstrate their skills. "We're looking for behaviors such as selling orientation, persuasiveness, interpersonal flexibility, enthusiasm, service orientation, organization skills, telephone communication skills, ability to retain information and ability to apply reasoning to particular situations," Wilson says. This exercise lasts approximately two hours.

"Realistic Job Preview"

If applicants successfully pass the simulation hurdle, the final phase is to send them onto the floor in one of the telephone centers to spend time with current agents. "We call this a 'realistic job preview,' where they can see for themselves what the job consists of and talk with our agents. It gives them an opportunity to be sure they do or don't want to handle our calls for eight hours every day. If we get positive feedback from them, indicating that they're interested in employment, we will hire them," he says.

GEICO advertises for new-hires mainly through newspaper advertising, targeting bright high school graduates. "We don't sense a need for a college degree, and find that people with recent college degrees will want to move through the organization faster than we want them to," Wilson says. "We try to find people who will stay on the phones for two to three years, minimum, and not someone looking to be chairman of the board in six months. Some of our locations have more difficulty than other locations finding people to meet these qualifications."

GEICO, for the most part, hires agents on a full-time basis. "Since we're open 24 hours a day, seven days a week, we do hire a few part-timers because of some unusual shifts. But our business is complex — we can't have people working less than 20 hours a week." A particularly good source of employees, especially in some parts of the country, is women returning to work after raising families. "In many areas, the cost of living has risen so much that people feel the real need for two incomes. These women coming back into the workforce are terrific employees," says Wilson.

New-Hires Spend First Year as Trainees

Wilson and his office designed the training program used to train agents at all GEICO locations. "Each site uses its own personnel, such as its underwriting departments and policy-holder services departments, for teaching the technical materials. But the philosophies and designs are the same at each," he says.

The first six to eight weeks consists of classroom training, and is based on the field into which the agent is entering (sales, service or claims). It includes technical education and hands-on training for the telephone and computer system, emphasizing drills and simulations. "We use the 'triangle technique,'" says Wilson, "with one student on the phone as a customer, one student on the phone as an insurance agent, and the instructor on the phone to monitor the simulation. Ideal training class size is six to eight new-hires, with a maximum of 10."

After this initial training, an agent is classified as an "insurance counselor in training." The first six months is a validation period, during which time new agents are adjusting and "getting up to speed." During the following six months, agents receive intermediate training. "At the end of a year, a new-hire becomes a full-fledged insurance counselor, either in a sales operation or service operation," he says.

Career Paths and Educational Opportunities

An extensive career path exists within GEICO's telephone unit and within the company. When agents enter the organization, they are "insurance counselors in training" for approximately one year. Then, depending on whether they are in sales, service or claims, there are several layers or levels to which they might aspire. "At the end of a year, agents may choose to become a multifunction insurance counselor. This means if they are working in sales, we will crosstrain them in service; if they are in service, we will crosstrain them in sales, so that they can perform in a multifunction capacity. This allows agents to receive a promotion to 'senior insurance counselor,'" he says.

"Or perhaps they are on the sales side, desire to stay on the sales side and are very good at what they're doing. They can enter into a monetary bonus program that is tied to production." This allows GEICO to take advantage of agents' best skills and permits agents to develop themselves professionally. Wilson explains that another position level is that of senior multifunction counselor. These "senior all-lines counselors" qualify to serve in sales and service, and also cross over in products, such as automobile and property insurance.

A very successful academic program is available for GEICO agents who want to earn business-oriented college degrees. "If agents want to pursue a degree in economics or psychology or other areas related to the workplace, we will pay their college tuition. We want our people to aspire to college degrees and, if they have a college degree, they may work toward a master's degree or other professional degree, if they desire." Many full-time agents attend college classes before or after their shifts.

Wilson says that the GEICO's selection program nets approximately half of all applicants. "But we must be very selective because we realize these agents are the most important people in our company. Our customers never see or hear the rest of us. Our agents are the people with whom our customers must feel comfortable and satisfied."

Net Reps: Crucial Staff for Today's Contact Center

by Wanda Sitzer

Jupiter Communications, a media research firm that focuses exclusively on the Internet and other technologies, estimates that there will be 33 million online shoppers in the year 2000 and 61 million by 2002. Another independent research firm, Forrester Research Inc., states that by year-end 1999, a wave of lower-income consumers will become "e-commerce ready," as 50 percent of households own PCs and 29 percent go online.

The rise in consumers using online medium for shopping and service is a compelling reason to link your call center operation to the Internet and, even more importantly, to ensure that you effectively hire and train Net reps — the agents who handle your online transactions, including:

- Traditional email responses
- Automated email responses with agent followup
- Web "callbacks" to online customers
- Live text-chat sessions (interactive, email "conversations" with customers)
- Voice over Internet protocol (VoIP) calls (agents and customers speak via their computers while viewing Web pages)
- Web "page-pushes" (agents send customized graphical images that address customer's specific needs)

Net Rep Success Traits

If you're just launching your call center/Internet initiative and thought that you could simply promote or transfer your best phone agents — think again! Net reps aren't just new and improved agents; they're a different breed entirely. The following is just a sampling of success traits these online agents must possess:

- **Technology comfort and know-how.** Net reps must be adept at using search tools, browsers and other technology that links the agent with the customer. Fast and

Chapter 3

accurate typing skills are also essential.

• **Written communication skills.** Net reps must have the ability to communicate online where time is of the essence. This writing may be "live" (e.g., text-chat) and differs from traditional letter composition. Email might be better named "e-talk," as it resembles a conversation in its informal and colloquial manner. Yet, because email is indelibly etched on a page, agents must avoid bad grammar and misstatements that can be published in tomorrow's *New York Times*. Whether you have an interactive online catalog or simply offer email as a means to resolve issues or answer inquiries, the Internet has its own business rules, jargon and communication style. These rules and nuances are more important for Net reps than for anyone.

• **Netiquette knowledge.** Online writing necessitates that Net reps have an aptitude for knowing when to apply what standards for netiquette. Simply defined, "netiquette" is network etiquette — the do's and don'ts of online communication. Netiquette covers both common courtesy online and the informal "'rules of the road' of cyberspace," according to Albion.com, a San Francisco-based Internet reference publishing firm. You need to employ Net reps who have the right temperament for handling irate online customers, who may express their dissatisfaction by writing an all-caps message (the equivalent of shouting). Your Net reps need to both recognize the signals of a disgruntled customer as well as respond without "flaming back." It takes netiquette knowledge and perceptivity to communicate empathy when the voice isn't available to accompany the words and soften the customer.

• **Multitasking ability.** Net reps need to be able to simultaneously provide customer service, browse online and use traditional call center tools, such as scripting.

• **Flexibility.** Net reps need to be able to adapt to the changes your company will undoubtedly encounter as it shifts its Internet strategy along the way.

• **Analytical and judgment skills.** Eddie Bauer Inc., whose online catalog (www.eddiebauer.com), features an interactive virtual dressing room, names "perceptivity" as a key Net rep trait. Net reps are required to read between the lines of email messages. Customers don't necessarily have good writing skills, and agents may have to interpret what the consumer is really asking before responding.

• **Sales orientation.** Another important Net rep trait is having a knack for sales even in a service environment. An online study conducted by information service provider Intelli-Quest discovered that only one in five users who browse actually opens his wallet. It is essential, therefore, that Net reps have the sales skills necessary to move customers past the point of browsing to actually buying.

• "Wisdom." Online customers' expectations are often higher than other customers since they have chosen what they perceive to be a faster, high-tech medium for shopping and service. In turn, they expect quality, in-depth feedback, detailed product knowledge and quick responses from Net reps. It's important to have Net reps who can do more than simply reiterate what's written on your Web site.

Change Needed in Traditional Hiring Practices

Finding agents who possess these success traits requires a customized approach — a change in the traditional phone agent hiring practices. Yet, an Internet research study sponsored by Initiatives Three shows that, while most call centers expect different traits for their Net reps, only 36 percent use a separate hiring process to find applicants with those traits. Additionally, while most study participants use phone agents to handle Net activities, they do not consider written communication to be a major phone agent trait and do not screen for it.

Prior to beginning the hiring process for Net reps, we suggest assessing the traits required and then writing a job description that defines the specific Net applications you support (text-chat or email response, for example), on-the-job tasks/functions, and the quality/productivity objectives you've set for online transactions.

Screening Applicants Online

Once you've completed a detailed job description for Net reps, it's time to start recruiting. Consider posting job positions and applications on your corporate Web site and asking applicants to respond via email. Applicants who step outside the box and call to ask job-related questions may not be ideal candidates for the job, as they have revealed their preferred communication style — vocal rather than written. Phone call followups to an email response, however, may simply indicate thoroughness on the candidate's part.

Determine how effective and comfortable the applicant is using the email medium. Did she attach her resume using easily decipherable fonts and applications? Look for candidates who offer multiple ways of getting their documents to you (for instance, attaching resumes as separate files as well as pasting them directly in the e-message itself).

Call centers that screen online should acknowledge — via email — receipt of candidates' resumes within 24 hours. Candidates passing the "test" can be scheduled for an "interview chat" (using text-chat). Such interviews illuminate the Net rep's potential to communicate clearly online. To enhance your assessment of the applicant, ask questions that relate directly to the successful Net rep traits you seek and to your call center's specific needs. For example, look for:

- Ease of chat session and netiquette use
- Typing skills
- Ability to interpret your questions while online
- Appropriate paraphrasing or questioning
- Simple, concise style and answers

After this brief online exercise, finish the interview over the phone to test the candidate's speaking and listening skills.

Face-to-Face Interviews and Online Role-Plays

Successful Net reps do more than just establish and manage online customer relationships. They need to integrate well with your entire call center operation. That means responding to coaching, working well with peers and thriving in a new and changing environment. Thus, to enhance your success of hiring the right candidates, schedule a face-to-face interview with qualified applicants after the online/phone screening steps. Use this interview session to determine whether or not the applicant appears to be a good fit with your organization and whether or not their communication skills and personality match up with your specific call center culture.

A final role-play or "e-play" will help solidify your hiring decision. The role-play should simulate an actual online transaction scenario for the candidate to address in an onsite, online setting.

Training and Support to Meet Net Rep Needs

Some of your existing agents may not fit the unique requirements of an online culture. Give them every chance of succeeding by supplying them with the appropriate tools and training. Here's a sample training curriculum your center may want to consider to help develop successful Net reps:

- Our Company's Internet Strategy — Today and Tomorrow
- E-Commerce/e-Care Intro — What Is It and What Is Your Role?
- Our Web site and Our Online Competition — A Guide to Your Online Resource
- Netiquette — What You Can and Can't Write, Say and Do
- How to e-Talk — Writing Skills for Effective Online Communication
- Traditional Sales and Service Skills with an e-Twist
- Online Productivity and Results
- Customer Information Systems and Net Rep Practice

To help ensure Net rep success, network with call centers that have successfully addressed the staffing issues surrounding call center/Web integration. For example, you may want to contact managers at some high-tech and financial services companies that are making big strides in agent support on the Web.

Securing Success in Cyberspace

Just as emails and text-chat transactions are different from traditional phone calls, Net reps are different from phone reps. The e-commerce strategy in your call center is only as effective as the staff supporting that strategy. Deploying a formal hiring and training program for Net reps will help you to secure your call center, and your entire enterprise, in cyberspace.

Chapter 3

Don't Waste Resources Developing the Wrong People

by Laurie Solomon

How do you ensure that you have the right people to be developed? By improving applicant-interview practices. Traditional one-on-one interviews can be time-consuming and ineffective. The following recommendations are a proven alternative to the typical hiring formula.

Start with a Phone Interview

A phone interview needn't even be a two-way conversation; consider using voice-mail. When advertising, publish the phone number for applicants to call and introduce the job with a recorded message, addressing the key things you'd like the applicant to know. Then ask applicants to leave a message with their pertinent information and answers to questions, such as "What most interests you about this opportunity?" and "Which of your skills would be best utilized in this position?" Let's face it, if applicants don't sound good on the phone and can't sell themselves, you probably don't want them in your call center.

Invite Qualified Candidates to a Group Interview

When I was a call center manager, we interviewed as many as 25 applicants at a time, with two to four agents participating. During the interview, provide an overview of your company and the call center position. Next, pair applicants and have them interview each another for five to 10 minutes. Then ask them to introduce each other to the group. This helps to reveal applicant's questioning and listening skills.

Once the introductions are complete, conduct the question-and-answer session. Observe who participates and who doesn't. As moderator, ask some questions of your own, and be creative. Questions like "Can you please give me the driving directions from your neighborhood to your favorite place to shop?" are very enlightening. Does

Chapter 3

the applicant provide clear and detailed information? Afterward, meet with your team members to compare notes and decide who to ask back for a second interview.

Invite Standouts to Come Back; Take Them "Where the Action Is"

Begin the followup interview as a group session again, but this time let the applicants introduce themselves. Initiate group discussions to see how applicants interact with one another. Ask them to respond to questions, such as "If you could change anything about your last/current job, what would it be?" and "Did you attempt to make such changes?"

Next, take all applicants into the call center. Pair each applicant with an experienced agent. Give them a headset and let them listen to calls for at least 30 minutes. Encourage applicants to ask agents questions between calls.

Once they've had time to observe agents in action, you can conduct your traditional one-on-one interviews. Also, get feedback from your experienced agents. This not only provides you with a fresh perspective of applicants, it gives your staff some "ownership" in the hiring process.

With turnover being one the greatest challenges for call centers, it's crucial to do all you can to get the right people with the right attitude and right commitment before training commences.

Tips for Creating a Proactive Development Program

1. **Attract them early.** High school and college internship programs are a great way to assist with the workload, while developing skills in potential future permanent employees.

2. **Make it easy to work for you.** Consider a satellite location on or near a college campus to attract part-time employees.

3. **Recognize and accept that you may need to continue the employee's basic education.** For example, by providing training for writing skills.

4. **Continue development at the individual's pace.** Independent self-paced learning utilizing technologies, such as the Web, intranet and CD-ROM, assures that we don't force more progressive employees to wait for a full class roster.

5. **Challenge internal attrition.** The concept of the call center as a training ground for the rest of the organization must be balanced. Sure, it can be good for the company, but constantly stripping the call center of experience is damaging to the customer and to the image of the call center in the organization.

6. **Make the call center a career-advancement step.** Promote from other departments within the organization.

7. **Make use of firsthand knowledge.** Those with the extensive practical knowledge gained from handling calls can be developed to populate knowledge-based systems as the subject matter experts.

8. **Organize for trends in customer contact.** Today, staffing is generally organized around channels of communication, with designated groups handling inbound calls, email, faxes and mail. While that may serve the call center's current needs, this will need to change as multimedia queues progress. Multiskilled groups provide development opportunities for the agents and for their leadership.

Chapter 3

Chapter 4:
Developing New-Hires
into Successful Agents

Ensuring New-Hire Success via "Transition Training"

Arrowhead Water's Innovative Hiring and Agent Development Practices

Agent Partners Tackle Training Challenges at Today's Merchandising's Call Center

Getting Aggressive with Agent Retention

Ensuring New-Hire Success via "Transition Training"

by Dan Lowe

One of the biggest challenges facing call center managers is quickly turning new-hires into effective agents. All too often, new-hires go through an initial training session and are then thrown on the phones where they receive little or no direct support while handling calls. This is the equivalent of showing a new swimmer how to swim, handing them instructional manuals, then sending them to their first race. It's no surprise that call centers that take such an approach often suffer high turnover right after training.

To avoid the "sink or swim" problem and help battle early attrition, many call centers have successfully implemented a "transition training" program as a part of the new-hire training process. Transition training enables new-hires to "do the job" while still in a nurturing learning environment. It involves having trainees — who've completed or nearly completed the classroom training — handle live calls from customers in a separate area in the call center under close supervision. The transition process can take anywhere from a few hours to several weeks, depending on the complexity of the agent's role in the call center.

This article will discuss how to determine if a transition training program is right for your call center, describe how to implement a successful program, and provide examples of actual call centers that have already done so.

Time for a Transition?

Answering the following questions can help you determine whether or not your call center could benefit from a transition training program:

- Are many new-hires who have successfully completed training struggling on the phones?
- Is early agent attrition excessive in the call center?
- Are frontline supervisors spending most of their time working with new agents?

- Are trainees fired up and ready coming out of training, only to quickly become frustrated and stressed out after a few days on the phones?

If you answered "yes" to any of these questions, a well-implemented transition training program could be just what your center needs.

Effective transition training programs provide numerous benefits:

- Trainers can better assess individual knowledge and phone skills before placing new-hires on the phone floor. Trainees who aren't "cut out" for the agent job are quickly identified and can be reassigned if necessary.

- Trainees develop a more thorough understanding of processes, information systems, products and services, as well as the confidence needed to succeed on the phones.

- New agents see the extra support the center gives them and thus feel valued, which results in increased motivation, higher morale, lower turnover and better service/customer satisfaction.

- Supervisors on the phone floor receive better-qualified trainees who require less supervision and coaching, freeing supervisors to focus on other key tasks.

- The program can be used to develop senior agents into effective supervisors by involving them in supervisory roles in the controlled call environment, where mistakes aren't so costly.

Implementing a Positive Program

Once you've decided that transition training is appropriate for your center, follow these steps to ensure a successful program:

1. Set and communicate clear objectives. Ensure that everyone involved — trainers, trainees, supervisors and even existing agents — understand the primary objectives of the transition training program. Explain how it is intended to provide trainees with an opportunity to integrate the skills and knowledge they've acquired from the classroom training in a supportive environment, where they can ask questions, make mistakes and begin to see how everything they've learned fits together.

2. Determine types of calls handled, skill-sets required and training timeframes. Decide exactly what kinds of calls will be routed to trainees "in transition"; what skills, product and systems knowledge trainees need to have prior to handling those calls; and, finally, how long transition training will last.

Some call centers divide transition training into segments, where the trainee practices handling certain call types/skills in the controlled environment, heads back to the classroom for additional instruction, then goes back on the phones to practice handling the new call types/skills.

Note: In many cases, the addition of a transition process to the new-hire training program enables call centers to reduce the classroom time by 10 percent to 30 percent — the reason is that agents often learn key "classroom" concepts while on the phones during transition training.

3. Create a "transition bay." The transition bay — or "nesting area" as some call centers call it — is where trainees handle calls prior to jumping out onto the official phone floor. The primary requirement for the transition bay is that it provides trainees access to the same telecommunications and informational systems that the existing call center agents have. The transition bay need not take space on the phone floor; it can be set up in virtually any room. Focus on replicating the "true calling environment" as closely as possible.

4. Select trainers/supervisors to oversee the transition bay. This is one of the most critical aspects of implementing a successful transition training program. It's essential to carefully choose the right people with the right skills to coach and nurture new-hires on the phones for the first time. Select transition bay supervisors from your pool of trainers, floor supervisors and senior agents. Look for candidates who are patient, and have strong knowledge of all call types and a proven ability to provide positive feedback.

The agent-to-supervisors ratio should be lower than it is on the official phone floor. While a 15:1 agent-to-supervisor ratio may suffice for experienced agents in the call center, a 5:1 or 7:1 ratio may be necessary in the transition bay to provide the immediate support that trainees need to develop the skills and confidence to succeed in the center.

Chapter 4

What Is the Cost?

Yes, there are costs associated with implementing an effective transition training program. These costs are associated with lengthening the overall training process, with using supervisory staff in the process, with using floor space as a transition bay, etc.

But consider the costs of not implementing a transition program: The cost of re-hiring and retraining due to high agent turnover; the costs associated with constant errors and rework caused by unprepared agents; the costs of missed sales opportunities; and the costs of poor service and lost customers.

Sample Programs

Company A, below, and Company B, on page 89, are two examples of actual call centers that have successfully implemented a transition training program.

Company A

1. Classroom training (two weeks)

2. Transition training (two weeks)

- A trainer and coaches support, monitor and give feedback to trainees in separate transition bay.
- Features a 3:1 trainee-to-supervisor ratio.
- Calls are segmented for the application(s) on which agents have been trained (i.e., billing calls).
- Trainees are occasionally brought back into the classroom to complete relevant modules.

3. Additional classroom training (three weeks)

4. Additional transition training (three weeks, or as needed)

- Trainees take a variety of general calls under close supervision.
- Training time is based on individual goal attainment and proficiency.
- Transition support staff report trainee's strengths and weaknesses to floor supervisor upon completion of training.

Chapter 4

Sample Programs

Company B

1. Classroom training (two weeks)

2. Transition training (two to four weeks)

- Training takes place within assigned "production" team.
- A supervisor, senior agent and other team members provide general support.
- Each trainee is assigned a mentor.
- Trainees practice approximately 20 percent of the total agent responsibilities.

3. Additional classroom training (two weeks)

4. Additional transition training (flexible — based on needs of trainees)

- Trainees return to assigned team.
- Receive daily feedback from support staff/mentor.
- Trainees practice a higher percentage of total agent tasks.
- Goals and objectives are geared to needs of individual trainees.

Chapter 4

Arrowhead Water's Innovative Hiring and Agent Development Practices

by Julia Mayben

In the current tight labor market, finding and keeping good agents is an ongoing battle for many call centers. But that's not the case at Arrowhead Water. In recent years, its Brea, California, call center has boasted an extremely low agent attrition rate of 10 percent annually, and the center's recruitment files are brimming with applications from candidates eager to work at the center.

Is it something in the water? Not exactly, says Jim Maguire, manager of the center, which handles sales and service calls for the bottled water company. "Much of our success is due to our culture, which emphasizes treating people with respect and dignity. Plus we have a lot of things to offer agents that other companies don't, including a strong people-development process."

When openings do occur at the 60-agent inbound center, managers take recruitment and hiring very seriously. The process is extensive, with prospective candidates first undergoing a detailed telephone screening before being invited to the center for two days of interviews. "The time and effort is worth it because our company and the applicant are both making a big decision about whether or not the applicant will fit into our culture long term," says Maguire.

The center's current hiring program has been in place for nearly three years. Prior to that, the process was "not very in-depth and because of that, we were attracting people who could handle calls, but didn't always have the service and sales focus that we have now," recalls Maguire.

Seeking Staff with a "Servant's Heart"

On average, the center hires about 15 new agents each year to fill vacancies primarily left by agents promoted to other areas in the company. Since the center isn't forced to conduct mass hirings, recruitment can be done at selected times during the year. Maguire estimates that 95 percent of the people to whom the center offers a

Chapter 4

position accept the job.

The center looks for candidates who have two to three years of customer service experience and possibly some sales experience. A college degree and computer skills are preferred, but not required. "We want people who have a customer service orientation, or what we call a 'servant's heart,'" explains Robin Lyons, manager of the employee development team that conducts the screenings and interviews. "We value that over things that we can easily train, like computer skills."

Typically, four to five employee development team members interview each candidate who passes the initial phone screening. Each interview session lasts 45 minutes to an hour, during which team members evaluate candidates' customer service skills as well as their knowledge/abilities in other key areas including teamwork, problem-solving, issue ownership, follow-through and commitment. During this process, the team members use standardized questions they've developed from an intensive review of the characteristics of the center's top agents.

Following these interviews, prospective agents sit with a veteran agent in the call center for 30 minutes to listen in on calls and get a clear glimpse of what the job entails. These sessions also give the veteran agents an opportunity to learn about the candidates. "Often, a peer will see things that a manager might not," says Lyons. Following each sit-in session, agents fill out evaluation forms. Completed forms are reviewed by the employee development team, as is the information collected during the initial interviews. Team members discuss the merits of each applicant, select the finalists and extend job offers to the most qualified candidates.

Arrowhead's Successful Hiring Steps

1. Employee development team screens applicants via phone.
2. Team conducts face-to-face interviews with qualified candidates.
3. Candidates sit with agents to observe call-handling and to ask questions.
4. Agents fill out evaluation form regarding each candidate.
5. Employee development team discusses each candidate's merit.
6. Team selects finalists and extends job offers.

Chapter 4

Beginning the Call Center Journey

Arrowhead's new-hire training program is as intensive as its hiring practices. The program lasts 20 days and consists of classroom and on-the-job training. The first four days of training, called "Beginning the Journey," gives new agents an overview of the company's philosophy, history and financial status. Four days is a long time to devote solely to company business, Lyons acknowledges, but it is time well spent. "Our goal is to mirror our brand image with our customer service image. The only way to do that is for CSRs to understand the company and our culture," she explains.

On the fifth day of training, new agents begin the sales and service portion of the program, which lasts 16 days. These sessions take place in the classroom, on the call center floor and during site visits to Arrowhead bottling plants. The training covers product knowledge, systems and processes, and company policies and procedures. Employee development team members lead the training, with the help of selected senior agents who assist with one-on-one coaching. By the end of the training period, new-hires take calls while sitting with a senior agent to receive "the full gamut of experience by the time they hit the call center floor on the 21st day," explains Lyons.

Once initial training is completed, new agents are seated near veteran agents who can answer the rookie's questions when needed. The employee development team continues to monitor the new agents' progress and provides coaching for the next 90 days to help them achieve a service level goal of effectively answering 85 percent of calls within 20 seconds.

Eventually, all new agents are assigned to a team that handles calls from a specific Arrowhead marketing region. Each team consists of as many as 10 inbound sales and service agents as well as approximately five employees who handle collections, special billing and accounts receivable calls.

When not handling incoming calls, agents on a team complete paperwork, compile billing information and occasionally make outbound collection calls. Maguire has found that the team-based environment gives agents a better understanding of each team member's responsibilities, which enhances communication and customer service. The team approach also increases agent morale, he says. "People don't feel

Chapter 4

separated into different classes of citizenship when they work in teams. Plus it has given them other things to do besides handling the 80 to 100 calls they each take every day."

Ongoing Agent Development Fosters Positive Culture

Further enhancing agent morale and productivity is the center's ongoing training program. All agents receive three to eight hours of focused training each month. This training is divided into two sessions, which agents attend as a team. The sessions cover a variety of topics, including current advertising and marketing plans, as well as team performance issues and skills refresher courses.

The center's emphasis on continuous agent training and development is essential for maintaining its positive environment as well as agent enthusiasm, says Maguire. "We're committed to spending a lot of time, money and effort on developing agents to become the people who help define our culture."

To minimize the service level impact of having one team off the phones at one time, the absent team's calls are overflowed to other teams in the center. And management schedules the training sessions carefully. "We only hold them in the afternoons when call volume is slower, and we adjust the amount of training depending on the calling season," Maguire explains.

Although ongoing training sessions are held in the classroom, agents do more than simply sit and passively listen to lectures. "We know that, to be effective, these sessions need to be interactive and include role-playing and discussion time," says Maguire.

Leadership Program Paves Career Path

Arrowhead has also recently developed a formal "leadership program" to enhance agent career opportunities and retention. "We recognized that we have two kinds of employees: those who want to stay in the call center and do a great job," says Maguire, "and those who want to grow."

The formalized two-year leadership program is open to any agent who has worked in the call center for at least a year and performed well. Interested agents must complete an essay describing why they want to participate in the program and why they feel they are qualified. Maguire and the employee development team review each essay and select candidates.

Those selected for the leadership program spend two years learning each role in the center and work on several projects that test their initiative, time-management skills and creativity. For example, one agent in the program recently created an online version of the center's 300-page help manual, providing agents instant access to key information while on calls.

As they progress through the leadership program, agents spend less time on the phones and more time working on projects. "Early on, they spend about 50 percent of their time off the phones on projects," explains Maguire. "Toward the end of the program, they're off the phones 100 percent."

Once agents complete the two-year program, they're eligible for any frontline supervisory positions that become available. Having such career options is a big enticement for agents like Yolanda Henderson. "I wanted to do something beyond being a CSR, and this gives me that opportunity," says Henderson, a veteran agent who recently was accepted into the leadership program.

Arrowhead management views the program as a great incentive for agents to stay with the company. "Everyone has the opportunity to do something more," says Maguire. "We're telling people that they don't have to go elsewhere to grow."

Henderson believes agents in the center are getting the message loud and clear. "As long as you show interest and proficiency, the company will take care of you," she says. "That makes you want to stay here forever."

Agent Partners Tackle Training Challenges at Today's Merchandising's Call Center

by Julia Mayben

Training new agents is a centerwide affair at Today's Merchandising Inc.'s call center in Peoria, Illinois. In addition to receiving extensive classroom instruction from the center's trainer, all new employees are paired with experienced agents for nearly a month to help them get acclimated to the call center environment prior to going solo on the phones. For more than two years, the mentoring program — called "New Employee Partners" — has succeeded in boosting trainees' comfort levels and confidence while helping to form solid bonds among the call center's 49 agents. As a result, turnover has dropped while morale and performance have improved.

"Call centers are very unique places, and new employees need help in understanding the intricacies of such an environment," says Barb Mast, telesales manager at Today's Merchandising's Peoria center, explaining why the company introduced the New Employee Partners program.

In addition to helping new-hires adapt to the dynamic call center arena, mentors help reinforce the information trainees receive during the classroom portion of the four-week training program, which covers product and systems information, sales techniques and customer service skills.

Today's Merchandising is a retail outlet for manufacturers. The company buys products from a variety of manufacturers and resells them. As Mast explains, "We fill in the distribution gaps for manufacturers."

Capitalizing on Agents' Teamwork Tendencies

The New Employee Partners program was the brainchild of Olivia Turner, the call center's trainer. She initially came up with the idea when, as an agent in the center, she saw that her colleagues had an inclination to help one another. Later, when she became the center's trainer, she saw her chance to capitalize on the partnership idea.

Chapter 4

"I wanted to develop a more focused program for new employees by formalizing the process," Turner says.

Selling manager Mast on the program was easy. "The idea of training experienced TSRs to help train the new people, make them feel comfortable and reinforce information made sense," says Mast.

Turner reviewed the proposed partnership idea with Mast, and together they worked out the program's details. Once they had a plan in hand, Turner introduced the program to the full- and part-time agents in the center. "We explained the entire plan to them to make sure they understood why we were doing it, and what the roles and responsibilities of being a partner were," says Turner.

During those meetings, Turner also reviewed the selection criteria for agents interested in being partners. While experience plays an important part in the selection process, Turner and Mast also judge candidates on their past performance scores as well as more subjective criteria, like enthusiasm. "We look at how experienced they are and what their performance scores have been, plus we use our own judgment about how well we think they would do as a partner. It's important to consider their attitude and how well they can explain things," says Mast. The program currently features eight mentoring partners.

Once selected, mentors attend a 45-minute training session, led by Turner. The session focuses more on how the program works than on how to be a good mentor, says Turner. "These are experienced agents who we have selected carefully — we're confident in their ability to train others." During the briefings, Turner explains that the partner's role is to provide personal training that mirrors what the new agent receives in the classroom. She also trains each partner to be respectful of the center's service levels when working with new agents. "They are taught to adjust how much time they spend explaining information to their partners if there [are a lot of calls in] queue," says Turner.

Partnership in Action

New agents are assigned a partner at the beginning of the training period. Turner pairs people she believes will work well together. Occasionally, she will allow friends to work together as partners. "It makes the new agents feel comfortable," she says. "We've found that if the trainee isn't learning, they'll say so." Turner has never had to reassign partners due to personality conflicts.

During the first few weeks of training, new agents attend sessions as a group in the classroom, then go to the call center floor to sit with their partner and listen in on calls. The partner's role is to review items from each call with their trainee. "We're an extension of the training process," says Sue Stemke, a senior agent and partner. "I've got the training schedule so I know what they're learning. Plus, I will ask the TSR what they've covered so I can help reinforce the information." These initial partnering sessions are held regularly and typically last one to two hours at a time. On average, partners spend anywhere from five to 10 hours together each week.

Devoting that much time to on-the-job training can cause drops in the center's service levels. "You can tell when new people are out on the floor," says Mast. "Mentoring partners are still taking calls but the handling time is longer." As a result, Mast and Turner are careful when scheduling training sessions with the partners. "We try to do it at times when we are fully staffed," says Turner.

Later in the training process, mentors come into the classroom while agents are learning account information. During these sessions, partners pose as customers to help reinforce the information taught by the trainer. As Stemke explains, "We get on the phones and call the TSRs just as if we were customers placing an order. We ask them questions so they have to look up information." After the calls, mentoring partners review and critique their trainees' performance.

New agents give high marks to the role-playing exercise. "It enables us to get familiar with the call process," says Joanna Williams, a new agent who recently completed the four-week training course. "We get real-life examples that help us fine-tune our skills. I felt more confident that I could handle the calls after those sessions."

As training progresses, new agents help their partner in the call center with live customer calls. While listening in on calls, for example, new agents type in the necessary information on the data screen while their partner speaks to the customer. Later, trainees and mentors switch roles. "This gives [new agents] time to concen-

Chapter 4

trate on one call-handling task at a time," explains Turner.

By the fourth week of training, new agents are ready to talk to the customer and type in data while their partner listens in, providing assistance when needed. While this is taking place, Turner monitors the new agents and evaluates their progress.

Unbreakable Agent Bonds

The end of the fourth week marks the end of the "official" partnering sessions, but the unique relationship between new agents and their partners continue. For instance, new agents are often seated near their partners after they finish training to foster additional interaction and mentoring.

But new agents soon find that they can get help from anyone. Agents say the program has helped form a bond among all employees in the center. "I found that the first week I was taking calls on my own, I was excited and nervous," recalls Williams. "But I knew that, the minute I had a question, someone was there to help. It's like everyone is your partner. Everyone is willing to help."

This bond has helped improve employee morale, and management has seen other benefits since launching "New Employee Partners." For one, turnover among new agents has declined. Mast attributes this to the program's experienced partners who help ease the stress that many new agents feel when they start training. "When they discover they have to learn thousands of products from many different manufacturers, it can be overwhelming and even frightening," Mast explains. "There's a feeling of 'I don't think I can do this.' The partners help them overcome that and help instill confidence that they can do the job."

The partnership program has also had a positive effect on new agent performance. Mast believes that the program helps new employees focus on training. "The partners play a large role in getting new agents quickly up to speed," she says. "They get them to concentrate on what needs to be learned and keep them from dwelling on 'What have I gotten myself into?'"

Mast acknowledges that the partner program won't put an end to agent turnover or performance problems in the call center, but she's sure of the program's value. "It is not the 'be all and end all' solution," says Mast. "But we've found it is one of the most important things we are doing to help overcome problems in those areas."

Getting Aggressive with Agent Retention

by Jennifer A. Wilber

High agent turnover is a big problem at most call centers. Unfortunately, the problem is often chalked up to the "nature of the call center beast" by even the most well-intentioned call center professionals. This defeatist attitude is unfortunate, considering the effort and cost involved in hiring and training agents in the first place.

Dramatically reducing turnover doesn't have to be an overwhelming task. There are many actions call center managers can take every day to get aggressive with agent retention. The success of every inbound call center depends on experienced, high-quality frontline staff, thus the last thing any manager should want to see is any of those quality agents walking out the door.

Agent retention is affected by a number of factors over which call center managers can exercise ample control. This article summarizes what every manager can do to ensure that their valued agents stick around and serve customers well for as long as possible.

Develop Tigers During Training

A successful agent retention strategy begins on the first day of training. Remind trainees of the crucial role that agents play in the call center, of their intrinsic value to the organization. Inspire new-hires to perform right from the start.

During initial training, provide key background information on the call center, the company and its customers. Describe the agent's job in detail, including the exciting opportunities that lie ahead. The training program itself needs to not only cover the knowledge and skill sets agents need to succeed, but also to incorporate creative games and interactive exercises to help enhance learning and break up the monotony of the passive classroom setting.

Provide ample training time to enable trainees to effectively learn all aspects of handling calls for your company. Measure their performance regularly and provide constant positive feedback. New agents often resign because they are thrown on the phones before they've grasped the key aspects taught during training. These agents

Chapter 4

don't quit because they are lazy, rather they often lack confidence due to insufficient training practices. It is essential for managers to ensure that agents know how to effectively handle calls before agents begin talking to customers on the phones.

Maintain Consistency, Manage Proactively

Another key retention factor is to maintain consistency by having policies and procedures in place that every manager and supervisor follows. Agents become unhappy with their jobs and mistrustful of their manager/supervisors if they perceive that some agents receive preferential treatment. Ensure that formal, yet realistic guidelines exist surrounding key call center issues, such as attendance, adherence to schedule and call monitoring, and that these guidelines are fully understood by both agents and managers/supervisors. Inconsistent policies or subjective treatment invariably lead to high agent turnover in the call center.

Proactive management is also essential for improving agent retention. Managers who act only after major problems occur will constantly find themselves "behind the eight ball," resulting in hasty decisions and poor treatment of agents. Proactive call center managers take a more holistic and preventive approach — focusing on continual agent development and learning to avoid major performance problems.

Proactive managers incorporate two key practices into their management methods: 1) They actively coach and monitor all agents throughout their employment. Managers who actively search for ways to enhance agents' value and make them more successful will certainly reduce turnover. 2) Proactive managers serve as role models for staff. They are honest, energetic, accessible, and dedicated to enhancing customer satisfaction. Every action you, as a call center manager, take affects how agents perceive their job and their value. Managers who are courteous and patient will inspire agents to be friendly to customers on the phones and take time to help them with complex transactions/problems. If managers act tired, bored or frustrated, the agents will likely feel the same way, treat customers poorly and soon seek alternative employment.

Attack Retention by Customizing Agent Support

To be truly effective in battling agent attrition, call center managers need to consider the length of time that each agent has worked in the center, and provide the appropriate type of support. Managers should be aware of the specific needs of three categories of frontline employees: 1) graduated trainees, 2) new agents, and 3) veterans. This approach will enable managers to attack the retention problem head on and develop a team of quality agents who will stay on board for years to come.

Let's take a closer look at each employee category and the appropriate actions you can take to foster confidence, enthusiasm and a sense of empowerment.

1. Graduated Trainees: Graduated trainees are the people fresh out of training and on the phones. All managers and supervisors — not just the person who conducted the initial training classes — need to pay special attention to these employees. Keep in mind how the first day in a fast-moving, dynamic call center environment feels. Make sure these employees feel comfortable and are excited about being part of the agent team. Shower them with enthusiasm. Here are some specific tips:

- Take time to welcome them personally.
- Learn and use the graduated trainees' names whenever you speak with them.
- Give them a detailed tour of the call center and introduce them to other agents.
- Set achievable, realistic goals for the first day (e.g., taking a call with a smile, becoming more comfortable with call procedures, etc.), and reinforce those goals throughout the day.
- Provide praise and recognition whenever possible.
- Reassure them that they can do the job and that they'll be successful if they simply use what they learned in training.
- Take some extra time to role-play one on one or in small groups if any graduated trainees are having difficulties.
- Conduct an upbeat wrap-up meeting. Talk with agents individually at the end of their first shift and encourage them to ask questions. Review goals for the day and training topics.

2. New Agents: The employees in this category include agents who have been on the phones in the call center for anywhere from a week to a month or two. Very few

Chapter 4

people are "naturals" at a job; it takes time to learn the ropes and excel. New agents are often forgotten about whenever an even newer group of trainees graduate and hit the phones. Here are some suggestions to keep new agents from feeling abandoned:

- Sit down and talk with them informally, and use their names!
- Compliment any improvement since their first day, week, etc.
- Check in with them often and ask how things are going so far.
- Set achievable, realistic and increasingly challenging goals for the near future.
- Include those who have been there for a month or more in recognition opportunities and contests (e.g., provide certificates for "most improved agent," "friendliest agent," etc.).
- Recognize "mini-anniversaries," such as "happy first week" or "happy first month." Ideally, this should be done in front of other agents at shift changes, staff meetings, etc.

3. Veterans: These are the agents who have been with you for several months or years. While many of these agents perform very well, some may begin using incorrect behaviors as their performance goes relatively unchecked by managers/supervisors. Therefore, they must receive ample support and feedback. It is important to do everything possible to make them feel appreciated for their longevity, as they can be excellent role models for new employees. Here's some advice that works:

- Recognize their good performance regularly with tangible or intangible rewards.
- Involve them in agent training. This can include having them serve as model agents for trainees to "shadow" for a day or two, or asking them to give brief presentations in training classes on how to effectively handle certain calls. You may even consider letting your star agents help with the design of your training program.
- Meet with these employees to discuss career path opportunities and possible timelines.
- Ask them for suggestions for contest ideas, incentives, etc.
- Assess their performance regularly and provide salary increases when appropriate.

Chapter 4

- Set challenging goals for them with incentives.
- Acknowledge "anniversaries" of veterans ("happy six months," "one year," etc). Include a small reward such as time-off or gift certificates.

Not a Futile Endeavor

Enhancing agent retention is not a futile endeavor. Dramatic improvements can be made easily by paying close attention to agents' specific needs and learning styles, and by constantly reminding them of their value to the organization. Proactive call center managers who provide thorough training, maintain consistency, foster enthusiasm and treat agents as valuable individuals rather than merely the "people on the phones" will retain high-quality employees and ensure the call center's overall success for years to come.

Chapter 4

Chapter 5:
Recruiting and Training
Call Center Management

Developing Super Reps into Supervisors

Training and Support for Frontline Supervisors

Tips on Recruiting Top-Quality Call Center Managers

Developing Super Reps into Supervisors
by Ann Smith

Call center managers often assume that supervisory positions can easily be filled by one of the experienced call center agents who are eagerly awaiting a career path slot to open up. One day the new position becomes available and *bang* — super rep gets promoted to supervisor overnight. The person was a great agent, so he or she will be a great supervisor, right? Wrong!

Most often, the position must be filled immediately and there is no time to properly train the promoted agent. The new supervisor is given a three-ring binder full of outdated or obsolete forms with sketchy instructions. The new supervisor is referred to the library of supervisor training videos and books, as well as computer-based training modules, and encouraged to make use of these resources ASAP. Then the hectic days and chaos begin! Because the supervisor is ill-prepared to perform in the new job, everything takes longer to complete. Hours and days are wasted while the new supervisor tries to figure things out.

Often, supervisors lacking in training and development fall back on what they are comfortable with and proficient at doing, such as completing time cards. Perhaps he or she takes over a call from an irate customer instead of coaching an agent through the call. The supervisor was taught how to handle the call, but doesn't know how to teach the techniques to others. The new supervisor is "consciously incompetent," and the true function of the supervisor is not fulfilled. The supervisor suffers, his team suffers and the call center suffers.

What does the new supervisor need to function effectively? The requirements will differ in each organization, but the process for determining needs should include the following:

• Prior to filling the position, review the supervisor position summary. Assure that the expectations are clear. Include specific duties and responsibilities.

• Define the position requirements. Include skills, traits, attitude, competencies, abilities, etc.

• Translate the job requirements into a specific needs analysis (see the box, right).

• Assess the new supervisor's capabilities. Determine the gap between the job requirements and the new supervisor's skills and knowledge.

• Design a training program to fill the gap. The plan should be specific with goals and timetables and a method for determining proficiency.

Review the sample "Supervisor Skills/Knowledge Analysis" list in the box. It would take a new supervisor weeks to complete the required training listed. Remember, the strategy for any type of resource planning is to have trained individuals when you need them, not weeks later. You can shorten the supervisor training time by incorporating a great deal of the training into agent training.

Check off the training items that could be beneficial to staff

---

Supervisor Skills/Knowledge Analysis

Call center mission, vision, values

Call center objectives

Supervisor's role in meeting objectives

Team as a business unit

Time management

Delegation

Managing meetings

Conflict management

Performance evaluation

Applicant interviewing and selection

Diversity training

Career development (their own/employees)

Analytical skills

Customer service skills

Sales skills

Leadership skills

Negotiation skills

Listening skills

Presentation skills

Employee management skills

Quality monitoring

Coaching and feedback

Product knowledge

ACD report analysis

---

members while they are still agents. These might include customer service, listening and negotiation skills training, while interviewing and selection training would be given only to supervisors.

Next, prioritize all training checked by indicating whether it is "mandatory" or "voluntary." (Keep in mind that agents who enthusiastically sign up for voluntary training are the ones to keep an eye on for supervisory positions.) If you have varying levels of agents (i.e., Tier 1, Tier 2), you may want to further identify what training is available at which level. You will most likely have some training that is unavailable to Tier I agents, which then becomes voluntary at Tier 2.

Both Tier I and 2 agents benefit from additional training. This process provides an opportunity for Tier 2 agents to position themselves for promotion to supervisor. It also means less training will be required once an agent is promoted to supervisor. When a new supervisor is named and you go back to the original Skills/Knowledge Analysis list, there will probably be a few things on which he or she must be trained. But you will certainly be ahead of the game.

Training and Support
for Frontline Supervisors

by Dan Lowe

Training programs for frontline call center agents have evolved over time to include many of the important elements to help new employees succeed in this diverse role. Many challenges in the call center environment — including high CSR attrition rates and ever-increasing customer satisfaction expectations — have given call center managers the incentive to develop comprehensive and thorough CSR training processes.

However, few call centers focus adequate attention on high-quality training and development processes for their frontline supervisors. And yet, most managers would agree that in today's business environment of low unemployment, low job loyalty and high competition for qualified CSRs, it is critical that the frontline supervisors be strong leaders with the knowledge and skills to create positive circumstances in which agents can thrive.

How can you ensure that your supervisors have the tools they need to be effective leaders? Let's explore a proven supervisor development process.

Examine Your Agent Training Processes

You can begin by looking at agent training "best practices" as used by leading call centers. Figure 1 on page 114 gives a clear description of the most common phases of a typical training and support plan for frontline agents. It also includes the purpose for each phase of the training process.

New supervisors need a similar kind of developmental process in order to succeed and to help their teams to succeed. Too many companies make the mistake of assuming that a competent frontline agent can quickly (and magically) evolve into a successful supervisor. While the fundamental skills sets provide a good foundation, supervisors require additional management skills that are generally not accounted for in a formal training program. Figure 2 on page 116 lists a few of the key training areas required for both frontline staff and supervisors.

With this in mind, where does the newly promoted call center supervisor get the additional skills and knowledge needed to handle the normal daily flow of issues and situations? In most cases, the answer is "on-the-job training" or "learn as you go." New supervisors may be able to pick up bits of knowledge from more experienced managers (many of whom also learned through a hit-or-miss, inconsistent manner). But there is a better way!

Four Key Steps to a Supervisor Training and Support Process

You can use the frontline agent training process as a model to build a comprehensive supervisor training program. There are four steps recommended to ensure the success of the new supervisor:

Figure 1

Training Phases and Purposes for Frontline Agents		
Phase	Description	Purpose
1	Company orientation	Provide information about company, benefits, job expectations, measurements, etc.
2	CSR training	Provide general and then detailed information on specific tasks to be completed in position. Provide introduction and practice with tools, automated systems, etc.
3	Nesting	Provide time in production area with experienced CSRs as models. Provide closely supervised "on-the-job" training. Provide the opportunity to fail in a safe environment.
4	Monitoring/coaching	Observe CSR performance to provide feedback on specific performance-related behaviors. Identify negative behaviors that could turn into bad habits. Identify and praise positive and appropriate behaviors.
5	Performance appraisal process	Provide regular feedback using company performance management or appraisal format. Provide feedback in all major and important job performance areas.

• **Orientation.** New supervisors should be given some kind of introduction to the position. This can be formatted in different ways, but the main objective is to clearly identify the roles and responsibilities of the frontline supervisor. Human resources personnel and upper management can help to offer the right perspective for orientation.

• **Training.** The actual training process for supervisors should be conducted using a variety of methods (i.e., classroom, seminars, self-paced, mentors, etc.). The focus of the training should be to identify knowledge and skill areas that are outside of the frontline agents' knowledge and skill set. Many of the skills and knowledge areas listed in Figure 2 on page 116 should be included. Training in these areas is usually done by human resource professionals, training staff members, call center managers or other experienced supervisors. The best supervisor training programs also include situational role-playing. This gives the trainee a chance to use new knowledge and skills in a realistic, but simulated environment.

• **Nesting/shadowing.** Many call centers find that providing new supervisors with a "nesting" opportunity by having the person shadow or "co-manage" a team for a period of time can help to ensure the individual's success as a leader. Nesting gives new supervisors a chance to observe an experienced supervisor's work flow. They have the opportunity to review organizational and time-management practices, employee interaction skills and team meetings. The supervisors selected to be "shadowed" should be effective role models for the new supervisor.

• **Coaching and/or mentoring.** Every new supervisor should be assigned a mentor. This may be his or her immediate manager, but does not need to be. The role of the mentor is to meet with new supervisors on a regular basis for the first several months in the position, as well as making themselves available on an as-needed basis. Mentors provide experienced insights on any challenges faced by new supervisors, as well as counseling and career direction. It is best to have a formal process in place to ensure that all necessary ground is covered. In addition, supervisors should also be paired with a representative from human resources for staff issues. This is especially important for new supervisors who are learning policies and procedures connected with interviewing, hiring, performance management, disciplinary actions and termination.

Time Investment Will Pay Off for Managers

Developing a formal supervisor training and support process will require a time commitment from your company. But the benefits to this kind of comprehensive approach are significant. The new supervisor will be able to gain the necessary knowledge and skills to be successful and help his or her team succeed.

It's important to keep in mind that this development period is an investment that will be paid back over time. Supervisors who go through a formal development process will be far more self-sufficient and therefore require less time from call center managers or human resources in the long run. Think of it as a "pay me now or pay me later" proposition.

Overall, providing your supervisors with adequate training processes is as important as frontline agent development programs. Just as well-trained agents produce higher-quality customer interactions, well-developed supervisors impact both internal and external satisfaction.

Figure 2

Agent and Supervisor Skill Sets

Agent Skills
- Customer interaction
- Systems manipulation
- Basic problem-solving
- Teaming
- Company process knowledge

Supervisor Skills
- Customer interaction
- Employee interaction
- Communication
- Systems manipulation
- High-level problem-solving
- Team leadership
- Company process knowledge
- Company HR policies and procedures knowledge
- Decision-making
- Conflict management
- Reports and data analysis
- Monitoring
- Coaching
- Performance management process knowledge
- Employee motivation and recognition

Tips on Recruiting Top-Quality Call Center Managers

by Mark Craig

With all the hoopla about recruiting and hiring the best agents for your call center, little attention has been given to bringing the best managers on board. Sure, such positions can often be filled by in-house employees, but not always. Sometimes it is necessary to look beyond the walls of your company to find the person best suited to maximize the potential of your center.

This is not to say that companies should not make it a priority to identify outstanding employees on staff who are ready for new management challenges. In fact, I suggest implementing progressive career paths to provide motivation for agents and supervisors. Ideally, the best candidate is already working for you.

However, organizations that rigidly adhere to the policy of promotion from within may be missing opportunities to revitalize their call centers with fresh blood and new ideas. If the ideal candidate is not already on your payroll, actively seek out that person who is already working somewhere. This article will provide you with some helpful tips on finding the manager you seek.

Sell Your Center

Gone are the days when call centers did manager applicants a favor by hiring them. Call centers are booming today and skilled, knowledgeable applicants are able to carefully select where they want to work. The high demand for skilled call center managers means you first have to "sell" your company to them.

To attract and hire quality leadership, a call center must provide an attractive career opportunity. You need to have a good response to the question, "What makes your company different or better than the rest?" While management recruits probably won't actually ask this, it's the unspoken inquiry they will use to evaluate which call center will benefit from their skill and experience. Among the attributes candidates will be looking for are a positive work environment and challenge; recognition of achievement and contributions to the department; authority to make and implement decisions; and opportunities for advancement. If your call center has a favorable geographic location (i.e., Hawaii or Key West!), be sure to draw applicants' attention to that aspect.

Next, design all your recruitment materials around the positive attributes of the job/company. Incorporate these materials into your corporate Web site and newspaper/publication ads, as well as into the interview process.

Once you've highlighted the benefits of working for your call center, develop a detailed job description as well as clearly defined call center goals and objectives. These are the most important elements in any recruitment effort, and must be completed before you begin reviewing resumes. Think about exactly what you want out of the person whom you hire. Call centers with a clear understanding of what they are looking for will shorten the hiring process and reduce the number of surprises in the long haul.

Use the Web to Catch Valuable Applicants

Now you're ready to go "full throttle" on the Internet. Companies are rushing onto the Internet for two reasons. First, they believe that higher-quality candidates utilize Web technology. Second, they get instantaneous access to job candidates at minimum cost.

Call centers with success stories in recruiting quality management via the Internet use their corporate Web site as the focal point. Candidates who visit the Web site have better awareness of the job and of the company when they apply. The most effective corporate Web pages have their "career opportunities" icon clearly visible. In addition to listing the selling points of the job/company, the Web site should be interesting and entertaining. Be sure to include your corporate Web address on all materials that you send out.

In addition to focusing on your own corporate Web site, consider commercial recruitment Web sites that are set up specifically for job seekers and recruiters. Some of the organizations that provide resume and job databases, as well as storage of corporate Web sites, include Headhunter.net (www.headhunter.net), Monster (www.monster.com), and Job Options (www.joboptions.com). There are call center-specific Web sites that provide similar services, including CRMXchange (www.crmxchange.com), Incoming Calls Management Institute (www.incoming.com) and the International Customer Service Association (www.icsa.com).

An emerging trend in online recruitment is to post messages in places where the person not actively looking for a job will see it. CNN, *USA Today* and local newspapers offer banner advertising, with a custom icon that will link potential candidates directly to the advertising corporation's Web site. This banner advertising is effective because of the fact that, many times, the right person for a position is the one not actively looking to make a change.

Studies show that the best way to promote online media, such as your company Web site, is through traditional media. When you consider the fact that many people are now reading the newspaper online, listing corporate Web addresses in ads is a must. Other studies consistently show that graphics are a key feature of the best ads. Artwork attracts interest by emphasizing important features or by expressing corporate image more quickly, clearly and dramatically than words can. Choose illustrations that dramatize the atmosphere in your call center.

Search Firm Strengths

Executive search firms, especially those that concentrate solely on the call center industry, can serve as another effective recruitment tool. These search firms' databases are filled with profiles of call center professionals worldwide. Recruiters at executive search firms know of managers in the industry who are looking to make a change. Many of these highly qualified managers are difficult to find through any other recruitment methods.

The biggest advantages of using a search firm are the resources they can provide for you. Most conduct a thorough interview process, including reference checks, before sending you potential candidates. A search firm can also inform candidates about call centers that they might not know about otherwise. For example, a call center manager in Ohio may not know of a potential opportunity with a larger call center in Virginia.

The Intrinsic Value of Networking

Networking is another simple, yet highly successful, way to locate quality managers for your call center. By offering employees a finder's fee for candidates referred and hired, companies maximize their method of search and recognize the potential of the people who already work for them.

Networking through membership in call center and management associations can also be very effective in finding managers for your center. Quality people stand out in such associations, and meetings and conferences provide easy ways to meet them. It's a good idea also to organize formal discussions about call center job opportunities at association meetings to help uncover possible candidates. Ask members what recruiting/hiring methods have and have not worked well for them in the past.

Membership in some industry-specific associations (i.e., International Customer Service Association) serves as a passport to members-only areas of their Web sites. This opportunity will provide you with further access to quality call center management personnel.

Peering Beyond the Resume

Regardless of the recruiting techniques you use, the ultimate challenge is the always the same: determining if the person behind the glowing resume matches the requirements of the position. Can the accomplishments on the resume be measured by specific results? Do the candidates have hands-on experience with your type of calling environment? Are their personal and professional goals compatible with where the call center is headed? Why do they want to work for your call center?

These questions must be answered before you decide to whom you'll hand the call center reins. By effectively defining your call center and actively seeking the type of manager you need, you will significantly increase the chances of finding the best available person for the job. Effective recruiting for managers can take a lot of time and effort, but the reward of having a smooth running call center with satisfied staff and customers is well worth the initial investment.

Chapter 6:
Alternative Labor Pools

Goodwill Toronto Trains Disabled Workers and Youth-at-Risk for Call Center Careers

GSA Call Center Provides Meaningful Jobs for Workers Who Are Blind

Goodwill Toronto Trains Disabled Workers and Youth-at-Risk for Call Center Careers

by Julia Mayben

With the explosive growth of the call center industry in recent years, many companies are struggling to find skilled individuals with whom to staff their centers. In Toronto, Canada, where competition for qualified labor is particularly tight, Goodwill Toronto is answering the employment distress call for several area call centers. The nonprofit organization recently organized two unique training programs designed to prepare youth-at-risk and persons with disabilities for rewarding call center careers.

"It's a win-win situation for trainees and call centers," says Sharon Myatt, who, as manager of business and call center training for Goodwill Toronto, oversees the two programs. "It's a working solution to high unemployment among persons with disabilities and young people at risk. They get training for a career, and companies get trained, highly motivated workers."

The Call Centre Training Program for Youth, launched in March 1997, has trained and found employment for approximately 120 young people who were considered "at risk" due to their lack of education or their socioeconomic situation. The Call Centre Training Program for Persons with Disabilities, which has trained 43 people with a variety of visible and invisible disabilities, was started nine months later.

"We realized that persons with disabilities represented another viable group to tap into," explains Myatt, who helped organize both programs. "The employer-partners we developed for the youth training were supportive of doing a second phase, so we were able to immediately develop a similar model."

Myatt reports that 93 percent of the youth-at-risk program graduates and 100 percent of the disabled graduates are still on the job. And many of them have advanced beyond their entry-level position. "Several have received salary increases or been promoted, and a few have even won awards for outstanding customer service," she adds.

The programs themselves have been recognized for excellence as well. The youth program, for example, received Goodwill's International Award in 1997 for "outstanding community-based training" and has received an "A" rating — the highest rating possible — from the Canadian government.

Setting Students Up for Successful Careers

A large part of the programs' success is due to Goodwill Toronto's careful screening of program participants. "We don't want to set up anyone for failure," Myatt explains. "We want to provide training to people we feel are going to be able to succeed despite the barriers they are facing."

Lynn Minos, diversity manager for Scotiabank (one of the programs' employer-partners) in Scarborough, Ontario, believes that in-depth screening also prepares prospective students for the job ahead. "By the end of the process, they are prepared and capable to give us 100 percent because they have clear expectations of the job and the environment they'll be working in," she says. Scotiabank has hired seven Goodwill training graduates to date.

Potential program participants are referred to Goodwill from a variety of non-profit agencies or respond to Goodwill Toronto advertisements about the programs. Applicants undergo a five-step review process, developed by Goodwill Toronto, to determine if they are right for the training. As part of the process, applicants receive an orientation of the call center industry and general job responsibilities, then take an aptitude test. Next, they are interviewed over the phone by a Goodwill Toronto representative, and then interviewed in person. The final step is an interview with an employer-partner, where candidates receive an overview of the company and its call center operation.

Once they are accepted into a program, students are "pre-hired" by an employer-partner before they begin training, a process Myatt believes is an integral part of both programs' success. "Many have taken training previously but never got hired because barriers are still there. We didn't want to reinvent the cycle that both groups have faced throughout their lives," she explains.

The "guaranteed employment" is the best part of the Goodwill programs, says Angie Sciabbarrasi, a recent graduate of the persons with disabilities training and an agent at Royal Bank Direct's call center in Mississauga, Ontario. "I didn't have any call center experience, but I liked the idea that, when I got training, I could be assured of a job in which I could make a career," she says.

Employer-partners, which now number more than 20 and include a variety of industries in the Toronto area, receive the same intense screening from Goodwill Toronto as do program participants. "We don't want companies that simply want to fill positions with a warm body. We want businesses that really care about their employees," Myatt says.

Myatt meets personally with prospective companies to review the programs and introduce the Goodwill staff. She then visits companies' call centers. "I want to see that the employees have a nice working environment and that things like pay, incentives and benefits are satisfactory," she explains.

In-Depth Training Places Participants Ahead of the Game

At the heart of the Goodwill Toronto training programs is a classroom curriculum that covers technical and soft-skills coaching. The curricula for the two programs are similar and were developed jointly by Myatt, members of her staff and a steering committee comprised of representatives from several employer-partners.

The classroom portion of the training lasts 12 weeks for the disabilities program and eight weeks for the youth-at-risk program. Goodwill Toronto's four trainers, all of whom have previous call center experience, lead the classroom sessions for both programs. Sessions are held in two state-of-the-art call centers that were built using donations from Royal Bank. Typically, 15 people are in each class, though it's not unusual for Myatt to have a few dropouts each session. "We've had instances when people who begin training don't work out. We usually retain at least 13 people each session," she says.

Trainers cover customer service and sales techniques and computer skills as well as soft-skills training in areas such as assertiveness, anger management, self-esteem building and effective listening. During the final weeks of training, students begin handling live calls, which are routed to Goodwill from employer-partners' call centers.

Employer-partners give Goodwill's classroom training high marks. "When Goodwill students come to us, they're well equipped to begin our specific training program. In fact, sometimes they're ahead of the other new-hires, especially when it comes to phone skills," says Shamena Maharaj, a call center trainer at Royal Bank Direct, which has employed over 30 Goodwill training graduates.

Following the classroom training, students in both programs begin on-the-job internships at their pre-assigned employer. The youth-at-risk program features an eight-week paid internship, while persons with disabilities participate in a 12-week paid internship. During that time, they follow the company's training program just as any other new-hire would.

Two weeks into the internship, Myatt and her staff begin periodically monitoring students' progress. "We go out to make sure everything is going well, and if there are any issues, we try to resolve them," says Myatt. Additionally, Myatt and her team receive a report from the employer on each student's progress to help pinpoint any problems. "For instance, one youth participant who went to Royal Bank had trouble grasping product information, so our trainer gave him special one-on-one coaching. Now he's doing a great job. Sometimes a little nudge is all that's needed," Myatt explains.

Graduates who successfully complete their internship go on to full-time employment with the call center where they interned.

Overcoming Assimilation Obstacles

Despite the programs' thoroughness, call center managers often encounter challenges assimilating Goodwill training graduates into their operations. Technology issues for persons with disabilities, for example, posed a problem for Lorie-Anne Faigal, manager of the electronic banking call center for Scotiabank. She oversees two visually impaired graduates from the Goodwill program. "We had to spend a lot of time making sure their data-reading devices worked with our system," she recalls.

The data-reading tool the center employs — called JAWS — is a voice-activated software program specifically designed for the visually impaired. The software takes written data and converts the material into verbal text, which the user then hears through earphones.

Faigal had a few other issues to work through, such as making sure the visually impaired agents had access to the same information other agents had. Because much of the material agents have is written, Faigal decided to hook up text scanners to the two agents' data readers. She also converted the written reports that all agents receive, such as performance appraisals, onto cassette tapes so the visually impaired agents could review their progress.

Cheryl Trebenski, a call center manager at Royal Bank Direct, was concerned that Goodwill's disabled graduates might not "fit in" at the call center. "We didn't want them to feel different from the other agents," she says. Initially, she considered conducting sensitivity training for agents who would be working with the Goodwill graduates, but found it unnecessary. "There weren't any real adjustments needed by agents on the floor. The Goodwill individuals had such great attitudes and fit in very well. The only real adjustments we made were to the workstations to accommodate their disabilities."

"Alternative" Labor Pool Offers Unlimited Opportunities

Trebenski believes that all call center professionals should consider tapping into the youth-at-risk and disabled labor pool. "I don't see what the limitations are. You get qualified employees who are committed to their job and interested in making it their career," she says.

Right now, Goodwill Toronto has no plans beyond continuing its two entry-level call center training programs. However, expansion of the programs may come from other Goodwill organizations around Canada and in the United States. "We've had other offices visit us and tell us that they would like to adapt the programs to their needs," says Myatt. "It's such a great idea, I wouldn't be surprised if it spread all over."

Chapter 6

GSA Call Center Provides Meaningful Jobs for Workers Who Are Blind

by Greg Levin

The General Services Administration's (GSA) Customer Supply Center in Franconia, Virginia, provides more than efficient and pleasant service to callers. Operated by the Virginia Industries for the Blind (VIB), the center also provides workers who are blind with challenging and fulfilling employment opportunities.

The GSA call center is staffed primarily with blind agents, who handle orders for office supplies and cleaning products for federal government agencies in the Mid-Atlantic region of the United States, including Virginia, West Virginia and Maryland.

"Many blind people have a difficult time finding meaningful jobs," says Karen Van Riper, vocational rehabilitation coordinator for VIB. "New technology and training has opened some employment doors, but it's still difficult. Fortunately, GSA has discovered that call center/customer service work is ideal for blind people seeking meaningful jobs."

GSA began staffing the Franconia center with blind phone agents in 1994. When the U.S. government started a hiring freeze, GSA, like many other federal agencies, decided to contract out several jobs, including those in the call center. The agency was familiar with the VIB and realized that the call center could provide blind people with good jobs. Rather than contract out the entire call center to the VIB initially, GSA and VIB implemented a pilot project in December 1994 involving five reps who were blind. The pilot, which lasted four months, was a success and VIB gradually took over the entire call center operation over the next several months.

"Once the pilot began, we realized it was going to work very well," says Skip Duncan, deputy assistant regional administrator for GSA in Washington, D.C. "VIB had done an excellent job of supplying well-trained agents who were able to provide, and even exceed, the quality of service we expected. As a result, we promptly decided to expand the pilot." The GSA employees who had been working in the call center were reassigned to other departments within the agency.

Today, 13 blind agents work in the call center, which has a total of 18 agent positions. The center is open from 7:30 a.m. to 4 p.m., Monday through Friday, and receives roughly 700 calls a day. During busier periods, some or all of the remaining five positions are staffed by temporary workers who are not blind. "Some of the jobs are visual, such as handling faxes, so it helps to have some employees who are not blind," Van Riper explains.

VIB is one of 87 agencies associated with the National Industries for the Blind (NIB), a federally funded agency headquartered in Alexandria, Virginia, whose goal is to enhance the opportunities for economic and personal independence of people who are blind. VIB is an independent organization, part of the Virginia Department for the Visually Handicapped (VDVH).

Unique Technology and Listening Skills

The 13 full-time agents in the GSA call center are all at least "legally" blind, meaning that their vision is 20/200 or worse in their best corrected eye. "You are considered legally blind if 20/200 is the best vision you have while wearing glasses with the strongest prescription possible," explains Van Riper. Many of the reps at the center, however, have much worse vision, including five who are totally blind.

VIB supplies all the necessary adaptive equipment and technology that the agents need to do their jobs.

Some reps use magnifying devices to read their computer screens or faxes; others require large monitors with 20- to 21-inch screens and enlarged-text capabilities. "The text on these machines is about one-quarter-inch high," says Van Riper. "That's really all that legally blind reps need in the way of adaptive technology."

The agents who are totally or nearly totally blind use more complex technology that enables them to handle calls effectively and efficiently. Their computers are loaded with software that features a speech synthesizer that reads everything on the computer screen out loud to the agents through a headset. The computer voice tells them not only which screen they are on, but also what they are typing so they can hear if they make a mistake. While this technology aids call-handling, it hardly makes it easy. During a call, agents hear the computer voice in one ear and the customer's voice in the other. "It's really tough," says Van Riper. "They have to learn to discriminate between the two voices — often the computer and the customer talk at the same time." Occasionally the agents have to ask a customer to repeat something, but most adapt to the technology quickly, she says.

One agent, Yosef Getachew, has overcome an additional obstacle. In addition to being totally blind, he's partially deaf and must listen to the customer and the computer in one ear! "I'm truly amazed how he does it," Van Riper says. But for Getachew, who's been working at the GSA call center for two and a half years, it's all just part of the job. "It's not that difficult, really. It's just something you have to get used to," he says. "It was kind of hard when I was first learning, but I've adapted very well."

Other specialized technology in the call center includes a Braille printer that converts regular text documents to Braille. "If there is a flyer or a memo that needs to go out to agents, we just type it into the computer and print it on the Braille printer," explains Van Riper. "We can also scan an existing document, and it will print in Braille."

Intense Training Helps Overcome Obstacles

Training for agents is intense, particularly for those with severely impaired vision. These agents have to learn how to use the speech technology in their computers as well as the order-entry system that all agents in the center use. Each agent also receives comprehensive customer service and office procedure training.

Van Riper conducts most of the training, which, because of the agents' varying levels of vision, is done one on one. Some of the technical training, such as basic computer skills, may be conducted at VDVH's rehab facility in Richmond, Virginia. Total training time required varies from agent to agent. "It depends on the agent's skill level and how quickly he or she adapts to the new technology," says Desi Campbell, the call center's supervisor, who assists Van Riper with much of the training.

Training times have shortened over the past year, says Van Riper, because most of the agents the center now hires already have good computer skills and are familiar with the adaptive technology. "Today, there are more places where blind people can receive general technical training to help prepare them for jobs," she says. "This makes it easier for us to find qualified agents."

The call center uses several methods when recruiting new agents. VIB first contacts its parent agency, VDVH, to tell them about any job openings. VDVH then contacts its six regional offices to see if they know of anybody who is qualified for and interested in working at the call center.

The center doesn't rely solely on regional searches when recruiting new agents. It often receives assistance from NIB, which has a national database of qualified workers who are blind. "NIB has a person who does a lot of job searching and development," Van Riper explains.

The center also lists job openings in publications that are provided by such organizations as the National Federation for the Blind and the American Council for the Blind.

All interested applicants send a resume and an application to VIB to be reviewed by Van Riper. When evaluating applicants, she looks for good computer and communication skills, as well as any customer-contact experience. Qualified applicants are brought in for an interview and those with the strongest skills are offered jobs.

Little Trouble with Transportation

While transportation to and from the call center can pose a challenge for the blind agents, tardiness/absenteeism is seldom a problem. Most of the agents use a door-to-door transportation system called Metro Access, which services disabled people throughout Washington, D.C., Northern Virginia and parts of Maryland. "The service is pretty reliable," Van Riper says. "Once in a rare while, Metro Access will forget to pick up one of our agents and he or she then has to scramble to get a cab to get to work on time. But I don't think we have any more of a problem with absenteeism than any other call center does."

A few of the agents who are not totally blind use the regular Metro system, which has a stop located about one mile from the GSA building that houses the call center. Other agents live close enough to the center to walk, and some have family members take them to and from work.

Allowing blind agents to work from their homes has been discussed, but such a telecommuting arrangement is unlikely to happen soon, according to Campbell. "The GSA isn't really interested in telecommuting at this point," she says. "Besides, as convenient as it would be for the agents, I think it's even more important for them to experience the social aspect of being in an office working with a lot of people. It also gives them the chance to meet and talk to people with similar challenges and problems."

Turnover Low, But Welcomed

Although the center doesn't track its turnover rate, Campbell estimates that it's probably lower than average because blind people don't have as many quality employment opportunities and are thus not as likely to leave after short stints. But the agents hardly feel stuck in the call center. They stay because they are treated well and like the work, says Van Riper. "They are paid well and receive good benefits, and the work itself is fulfilling and fun."

Agent Getachew couldn't agree more.

"I'm not going to say it's an easy job, but it's a rewarding one," he says. "The call center has been very helpful in providing the equipment and the training I've needed. Everybody is very supportive and makes me feel like a valued employee."

Campbell is glad that most agents feel the same way, but she realizes that some agent attrition is important. "We don't expect every agent to stay with us forever," she says. "We want them to improve their skill levels in the call center and evolve. We provide a great opportunity for blind people to gain a lot of knowledge and experience that can help them move on in their careers." Several have moved on to other good jobs, including one agent who recently took a position as a marketing representative for NIB.

Steering Past the Stereotypes

Part of the call center's mission is to educate other employers about the capabilities of many blind people, says Van Riper. She feels that stereotypes prevent many companies — including call centers — from hiring blind workers for important jobs.

"I've found that a lot of people think blind people must be unintelligent because they can't see," she explains. "Employers need to understand that blind people have the same normal curve of characteristics as any group of people — some are smart, some are not so smart; some are nice, some are not so nice; some are ambitious, some are not so ambitious. I can tell you that we have wonderful agents here who are very skilled, highly motivated and do a fantastic job. I'm not saying that they are skilled, motivated and do good work considering the fact that they are blind; they do as great a job as anybody could."

Chapter 7:
Hiring Humor

Effective Pre-Employment Questions

Separating the Reps from the Replicas

Effective Pre-Employment Questions
by Greg Levin

Agents are a call center manager's most vital tool. In fact, a recent paramount study conducted by a prestigious research firm revealed that phone reps, more than any other single factor, are what keep a call center's headsets from simply falling to the floor. Phone reps — not technology — also provide the quality customer service that keeps your customers coming back (with the possible exception of one church call center that has as its VRU message, "God loves those who don't jam up queues. Be an angel and call us later.")

With phone reps playing such an important role in the success of your call center, it's essential that you take the time to hire the right people. Too many call center managers, anxious to get coverage for the phones, rush through the agent-selection process. These managers then act surprised when they later find out the person they hired is either unqualified, unreliable, noncooperative or, worse yet, not a person at all, but rather a giant lizard with a good makeup job.

To ensure that the agents you hire are the cream of the crop, ask every applicant the following two multiple-choice questions and evaluate each candidate based on the comments provided. I guarantee you that incorporating these two questions into your hiring procedures will yield a vast improvement in the quality of people you bring on board over the next year. If you are not completely satisfied with the results in 12 months, simply send me the unused portion of the questions in their original wrapper along with an explanation as to why you are not satisfied, and I will promptly send you a tasty garden salad and some yarn.

1. What's the primary reason you want to work as a phone rep in this call center?

a. I think it would be an interesting and challenging opportunity to help me develop my customer service and problem-solving skills, and may lead to a promising career in management.

b. The call center industry is an emerging field and I very much want to enter into

Chapter 7

it via your organization.

    c. The voices in my head keep telling me it's the right thing to do.

- Be wary of applicants who choose 'a,' as they are probably tremendously egotistical and pushy. "Oh, I'm great. I've got skills." How annoying. They haven't even been offered a position and already they are talking about running the show.

- Those who choose 'b' are brown-nosers. They'll tell you everything you want to hear without any intention of staying true to their word. These people are the root cause of much pain and suffering in the world, and should be escorted out of your center by heavily armed security guards.

- Applicants who choose 'c' show creative potential and a propensity to break free from the norm, and may help pull your call center out of the rut in which it is currently stuck. Remember to keep an open mind. It's important to hire a diverse mix of people, including those who require a padded workstation free of sharp objects.

2. The most important thing to remember when dealing with angry customers is...

    a. To offer empathy and support, with such statements as "I see" and "I understand your frustration" and "If I were there, I'd hold you."

    b. That you are the person the ACD has chosen to take charge of the situation and to transform that caller's frown into a smile.

    c. That no matter how furious they are and how loud they yell, they're going to die some day.

- Those applicants who choose 'a' are the same people who always say that everything is going to be okay, even when you tell them that you have to move to Detroit. They are deceptive and dangerous. I not only recommend not hiring these types of people, but I suggest you immediately fire any existing employees who respond to this question in the same way.

- If you can honestly tell me that you want "everything-happens-for-a-reason" people working for you, then go ahead and hire applicants who choose 'b.' But be warned, these people will use the concept of "fate" to defend their every action in the call center. "Oh, I'm not sure why I called that customer a 'waste of organic material' and hung up on him. ... I guess it was just meant to be."

- Applicants who choose 'c' have the right idea. They are able to keep a level head in times of trouble and are less likely to burn out. In addition, their obsession with the futility of human existence often leaves them with few friends, which means they will rarely complain that the schedule interferes with their social lives.

Chapter 7

Separating the Reps from the Replicas

by Greg Levin

Every call center professional claims that they follow "best practices" when hiring agents, yet their turnover rates remain higher than their body temperature. I think it's time for call center managers to start taking some risks with regard to their hiring procedures. Asking the same tired prescreening questions — "Why do you want this job?" "What are your strengths and weaknesses?" "You smell great; what's that you're wearing?" — will result in the same tired, rehearsed responses that you've heard from agent applicants for years.

The best way to measure applicants' worth is by catching them off-guard during the interview process. The call center can be a hectic place with crushing call volumes, irate customers and coffee shortages in the breakroom, so you must seek agents who truly know how to handle unexpected adversity and think on their feet. Below are some suggestions on how to sift out Rambo reps from wimpy replicas during the hiring process.

• **Place the applicant in a room full of snakes.** This will enable you to see how well the applicant responds to extraordinarily stressful situations. Once you've placed the applicant in the snake-infested room, observe his or her behavior through a two-way police mirror. Applicants who merely huddle in the corner and shiver probably aren't the kind of folks who will be able to handle the phones during your peak season. Look for applicants who are able to overcome the situation by using their brains. Examples include applicants who get down on the floor and squirm to become "one" with the snakes, and applicants who calmly threaten to sue your company for millions if you don't remove all the serpents immediately. If your call center has a really high-stress environment and you don't feel the snake test is enough, try placing the applicant in a room filled with dentists or Gap salespeople.

• **Insult the applicant's mother.** After going over the applicant's resume and asking some preliminary interview questions, begin casting aspersions about his or her mom. This is a great way to measure how well the applicant will handle abusive customers. Remember, applicants who lose their temper with you — their possible future boss — are certainly likely to do the same with callers, and thus should be turned away. Applicants who respond to the insults by merely smiling and saying "I agree" probably aren't the best candidates either. Look for applicants who recognize that you've insulted their mother and who are willing to calmly discuss why you may feel the way you do. Example response: "I'm sorry that you think my mom bears resemblance to a bulldog with leprosy. Maybe if I had some more information I'd understand your point of view."

• **Tell them they can choose their salary.** By giving applicants such freedom, you can measure how responsibly they will handle empowerment. You want agents on whom you can depend to make important decisions with confidence. Applicants who respond to the "salary" question by drooling uncontrollably and yelling out "Papa needs a new pair of shoes!" probably aren't fit to work in a self-directed inbound environment, unless it's that of your rival company. Ideal candidates are those who choose a salary that's within $1,500 of what you have in mind. But don't forget to remind applicants who select salaries within this range that the whole thing was just an exercise and that they will be making $7.50/hour ($7.75 if they have a Master's degree) whether they like it or not.

• **Check for unusually large or small craniums.** This has little to do with the theme of this article, but it's still important. The cost involved in hiring and training new agents is high enough; don't make matters worse by selecting applicants who need custom-fitted headsets. Candidates with craniums smaller than 6 inches or larger than that of Jay Leno can cost your company a small fortune and thus should be weeded out during the screening process. But be careful not to put your company at risk for a skull discrimination lawsuit. For example, it's better to tell a small-headed applicant that he lacks the experience your call center requires than to tell him that you have a policy against hiring people with a grapefruit attached to their neck.

Final Note: Once you've narrowed the choices down to a few highly qualified agent applicants, make sure that you hire the most physically unattractive and annoying ones. The reason for this is that, if they truly are talented, they'll likely soon be stolen from you by another department within you company, and you won't miss them as much if they are ugly and irritating.

Index

Publication Dates

How to Reach the Publisher

We would love to hear from you! How could this book be improved? Has it been helpful? No comments are off limits! You can reach us at:

Mailing Address: Call Center Press, a division of ICMI, Inc.
P.O. Box 6177
Annapolis, MD 21401

Telephone: 410-267-0700, 800-672-6177

Fax: 410-267-0962

Email: icmi@incoming.com

Web site: www.incoming.com

About Incoming Calls
Management Institute
and Call Center Press, a division of ICMI, Inc.

Incoming Calls Management Institute (ICMI) offers the most comprehensive training programs and educational resources available for call center management professionals. Established in 1985 and the first to offer training on call center management, ICMI is a global leader in call center management training, publications and consulting.

ICMI's focus is helping individuals and organizations understand the dynamics of call center management in order to improve operational performance and achieve business results. ICMI provides high-caliber education and consulting to organizations ranging from small, start-up firms to national governments to multinational corporations.

Call Center Press, a division of ICMI, publishes the authoritative journal *Call Center Management Review* and the popular "how-to" book for call center managers, *Call Center Management On Fast Forward*.

A recognized pioneer in the field of call center management, ICMI is independent and not associated with, owned or subsidized by any industry supplier.

Visit www.incoming.com for more information on ICMI, industry resources, research and links, and to join a network of call center management professionals.

CONTACT INFORMATION:

Mailing Address:	P.O. Box 6177
	Annapolis, MD 21401
Telephone:	410-267-0700, 800-672-6177
Email:	icmi@incoming.com
Web site:	www.incoming.com (ICMI)
	www.ccmreview.com (*Call Center Management Review*)

Author Biographies

Mark Craig is a senior executive placement consultant with TeleDevelopment Services (TDS) Inc., an international call center consulting and recruiting firm located in Richfield, Ohio.

Leslie Hansen Harps is a freelance business writer specializing in customer service and call centers. She is the former president of the Customer Service Institute, and author of several books.

Greg Levin is the former editor of *Call Center Management Review* and author of the "In Your Ear" call center humor series. Greg is currently a freelance writer based in Spain.

Dan Lowe, president of Lowe Consulting Group, is a consultant and trainer specializing in call center development. LCG provides call center process assessments, including hiring, training, transition process and supervisor effectiveness.

Julia Mayben is a freelance writer based in Annapolis, Maryland. She is a regular contributor to *Call Center Management Review*, and is coauthor of *Call Center Management on Fast Forward*.

Bette Mock is the former cofounder and editor of *Service Level Newsletter* (now *Call Center Management Review*). She has studied call center management since 1983.

Anita O'Hara is vice president of customer service at Nextel. She has been in call center management for more than 16 years. She has held assignments with Urban Media, MediaOne, GTE Wireless and AT&T.

Wanda Sitzer is a co-founder and executive vice president of Initiatives Three Inc., a call center consulting company committed to elevating the practice and performance of call centers through branding.

Ann Smith is president of Dallas-based Smith Consulting and Training, an independent consulting firm specializing in call center management. She is a Certified Associate of Incoming Calls Management Institute (ICMI).

Laurie Solomon is president of LKS Training Services Inc., an independent call center training and consulting firm. She is a Certified Associate of Incoming Calls Management Institute (ICMI).

Jennifer Wilber is vice president of training and quality assurance for National Service Direct Inc., a call center services provider in Atlanta. She also provides the customized training design and facilitation for the Call Center Management Institute, a training and consulting service for call centers also based in Atlanta.

Order Form

QTY.	ITEM	PRICE
	Call Center Recruting and New Hire Training: The Best of Call Center Management Review – 150 pages, paperback – $16.95 each* *Multiple Publication Sales Discount	
	Call Center Forecasting and Scheduling: The Best of Call Center Management Review – 104 pages, paperback, more than 35 charts and graphs – $16.95 each* *Multiple Publication Sales Discount	
	Call Center Management On Fast Forward Book – 281 pages, paperback, more than 100 charts and graphs – $34.95 each* *Multiple Publication Sales Discount	
	Call Center Management On Fast Forward Book on Tape – $49.95 each	
	Call Center Management Review – monthly 20-page journal $337 (1-year subscription)	
	Shipping & Handling @ $5.00 per US shipment plus $1.00 per book/tape set and $.50 per software order. Additional charges apply to shipments outside the US.	
	Tax (5% MD and 7% GST Canada)	
	Total in U.S. Dollars	

*11-20 Copies (10% off) • 21-50 Copies (20% off) • 50+ Copies (30% off)

☐ Yes, please send me a free issue of *Call Center Management Review* and information on other publications and seminars.

Please ship my order and/or information to:

Name_____

Title _____Industry _____

Company_____

Address_____

City _____State_____Postal Code _____

Telephone ( ) _____Fax ( ) _____

E-Mail _____

Method of Payment (Check one)

☐ Check enclosed (Make payable to ICMI, Inc.; U.S. Dollars only)

☐ Invoice me

☐ Charge to: ☐ American Express ☐ MasterCard ☐ Visa

Account No._____Expiration Date _____

Name on Card _____

Fax order to:	410-267-0962
call us at:	800-672-6177 (410-267-0700)
order online at:	www.incoming.com
or mail order to:	ICMI, Inc. P.O. Box 6177, Annapolis, MD 21401

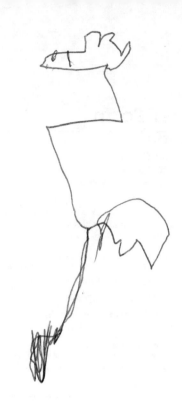